Kicking On

Laurie Berglie

Kicking On

This book is a work of fiction. Names, characters, businesses, organizations, places, events, and incidents are either the product of the author's imagination or are used fictitiously. Any resemblance to actual persons, living or dead, events, businesses, companies, or locales is entirely coincidental.

ISBN: 9781790319534
Imprint: Independently published
Cover Photo Credit: Tammie J. Monaco

For my grandmom, Helen –
From whom I've inherited my love of writing. Thank you for all the encouragement.

~ Chapter 1 ~

"Molly!" Macy exclaimed, "You look so beautiful!" She couldn't believe that her best friend was getting married today.

In front of a full-length mirror in her childhood bedroom, Molly stood in her wedding dress, grinning from ear to ear.

Molly blushed under Macy's compliment. "She's right, sweetheart," said Molly's mom, Karen, as she walked over and put her arm around her daughter's waist. "You look absolutely breathtaking. Beau won't be able to keep his eyes off you." Her sister Erin nodded in the background. Overcome with emotion, she stayed silent.

Always simple in nature, Molly had chosen a dress that reflected just this. It was a strapless, off-white gown that daintily hugged her curves until it flared out just below her hips. Molly's light brown hair lay in tousled curls that had been pulled over to the right side in a low, loose bun, and her sun-kissed blonde highlights stood out. A daisy adorned that same side, and a strand of pearls around her neck completed her look. She had decided against wearing a veil. It was August, and she'd be hot enough without it.

Beau had proposed on Christmas Eve the previous year. Yes, they had only known each other for six months, but when you know, you know. Molly had always dreamed of a beautiful summer wedding, and they decided that early August would be perfect. With Karen's organizational skills and Erin's love of a good party, Molly knew they'd have no problem planning a wedding in just eight months.

"Okay, it's tradition time," Macy sang. Molly turned to smile at her best friend, her only bridesmaid other than Erin, the matron of honor. “I believe your mom has the *something old*.”

“Yes, I do.” Karen produced an exquisite pair of pearl earrings that matched Molly’s necklace. “These pearls were your grandmother’s; she wore them on her wedding day and would have wanted you to have them. I’ve had them reset in white gold so they’d match your wedding band.”

Molly gasped. “Mom, they’re gorgeous! I’d be so honored to wear them.” She turned back in front of the mirror and quickly put them in. They truly completed her look.

“My turn!” Erin had found her voice again and was standing there holding the *something new*. It was a small silver horseshoe hair clip. “I bought it at this cute boutique downtown.” She clipped it just behind Molly’s ear, right beside the daisy. It was small, yet it glittered in the sunlight streaming in from the windows.

“Erin, I love it! Thank you!” Molly turned her head to the side so she could see it more clearly. She laughed, “You all know me so well.”

“I have the *something borrowed*,” Macy said, coming forward with a thin, silver bracelet. “My mom gave me this bracelet on the day I graduated vet school, and I know you’ve always admired it. And since you’re marrying a vet today, I thought it would go perfectly.”

Molly held out her wrist as Macy affixed the clasp. “Mace,” Molly said, placing her hand to her chest for a moment. “It is beyond perfect. I’ve always loved it. Thank you.” Molly was close to tears.

“Alright, last but not least, *something blue*.” Erin said with a wicked grin. She was holding something behind her back.

Molly stared at her sister. “Why are you smiling like that?” She asked. “What do you have?”

"Are you wearing underwear?" Erin asked.

Molly was speechless for a moment. "What? Of course!" She was afraid she knew where this was going.

With a Cheshire cat smile, Erin revealed a light blue, lacy thong. "Here, you've got to wear this one instead. It's light blue so the color won't show through the dress."

Molly blushed again as her sister, mother, and best friend shrieked with laughter. Without a word, she grabbed the thong from her sister and trotted into the bathroom to change. "If I didn't love you all so much," she called from the other room, "I wouldn't play along with this." Then she, too, started giggling. "It is really pretty."

When she re-entered the room, her mom was holding one last thing. "Don't forget the penny in your shoe!" Molly slid the coin inside one of her matching pumps and sighed happily. With all these good luck traditions accounted for, she and Beau should have a wonderful marriage.

Erin peeked out the window. "It looks like everyone's about here. Time to go get hitched, my love!" She and Macy both looked brilliant in their royal blue bridesmaid's dresses and summer tans. With their similar slim builds, they wore their strapless, tee-length gowns beautifully. Macy's curly blonde hair was piled high on her head. Erin's dark brown hair was swept up in a classic chignon.

With one final look in the mirror, Molly re-applied her lipstick and declared herself ready. She and Beau wanted a simple backyard wedding at her parents' farm. They would be married under the two hundred year old oak tree on the side of the yard that overlooked the horse fields. The reception would be held in a tent that had been set up behind her parents' pool area. Luckily, even though it was hot at ninety-four degrees, the weather had somewhat cooperated. It was sunny with low humidity and a light breeze was blowing. It was time to become Mrs. Bridges.

~~~~~

Macy couldn't believe how happy she was for her best friend. As she watched Molly and Beau exchange their vows to love, honor, and obey for as long as they both shall live, she wiped tears from her eyes. She didn't believe two people more suited for each other existed. Thank goodness Molly had come west to Kentucky for an extended break last summer and met the love of her life.

Beau, with his black tuxedo and black cowboy boots, looked stunning, but the way he looked adoringly at Molly with tears streaming down his face made him all the more handsome.

When the pastor announced that Beau could kiss his bride, Macy placed her pinky fingers in her mouth and let out the loudest whistle she could muster. Now it was time to party!
~~~~~

~ Chapter 2 ~

"Wasn't she just the most beautiful bride you've ever seen?" Macy asked her mother, Hadley, later that night as the two sat at her mom's kitchen table drinking mugs of hot tea.

Hadley nodded in agreement. "She absolutely was, though Erin was mighty pretty on her wedding day too. Those Sorrenson girls are blessed with good genes," she said with a smile. "Although I know someone else who will be a beautiful bride…if she'd ever find a man and settle down!" She stared pointedly at her daughter.

"I know, mom, I'm trying! I just don't meet a lot of guys these days. The ones at work are either married or too old. And when I'm not working, I'm hanging out with Hunter or sleeping. Eligible bachelors don't normally flock to dressage stables," she said with a grin.

Hadley understood. "I know, sweetie. I'm just giving you a hard time," she said with a wink. "I just want to see you married with a family of your own, but I guess I'll settle for my grand-horse for now. How is old Hunter these days?"

Macy lit up at the mention of her beloved horse. "He's perfect, as usual. You need to visit; I know he misses you."

"I do think a visit is in order. Maybe I'll come out sometime in September. It's been a while since I've graced the bluegrass with my presence," she laughed.

Macy laughed along as she poured herself another mug of tea. She loved coming home and spending time with her mom. Her brother, Tommy, and his wife, Cora, lived in the area, but Macy knew her mother was lonely from time to time, especially living in this old farmhouse on forty acres by herself. Macy had always wondered why her mother hadn't remarried. After all, her father had been gone for just over twenty years.

It had been a while since Macy and her mother had caught up like this, sipping their tea, and chatting way into the night. Macy told her mother how Molly and Beau had just settled on their new house two weeks prior to the wedding. Molly had given Macy a tour when she had first gotten into town three days ago. The house was a brick colonial on almost three acres. Since Molly and Beau planned to keep their horses at Molly's parents' farm, it wasn't necessary to buy a place with a lot of property.

The best part of the house, Macy told her mother, was the library that Molly had claimed as her office. It had built-in floor-to-ceiling bookshelves on two of the four walls, and it faced the back of the house where Molly could watch the deer and foxes come out of the woods at dusk. Macy got so excited thinking about the novels her best friend would write while sitting in that library.

"I'm so happy that Molly decided to stay in the area after all," Hadley said. "I was worried she and Beau would move to Georgia where his family's from. I know how glad Karen is to have her daughters close by. Tommy and Cora are just a fifteen minute drive south. If only I could get that daughter of mine to move back east," she said with a sly smile.

Macy smiled at her. "Oh, I'm thinking about it, don't you worry. My internship is up in December, and unless I'm offered an amazing position there, or if I meet someone, I'm heading home. Or at least back to the east coast. I love Kentucky, but I'm started to feel so isolated there. Absolutely everyone I love is here. Life is too short to be separated for long."

Hadley reached across the table and took her

daughter's hand. "Now that, my love, is music to a mother's ears. You do what's best for you, of course, but I'm not going to pretend that I don't miss you every second. I know you'll come home when you can."

~~~~~

"Molly, this just feels weird," Macy said as she placed her left foot into the stirrup and swung her right leg over the saddle. "You should be on your honeymoon, not horseback riding with me."

Molly laughed as she rode up alongside Macy. "It's okay. Since all of Beau's family is from out of town, we felt bad just taking off the very next day. We wanted to stick around one more day and celebrate. We'll hop on our plane to Mexico tomorrow when the Bridges clan heads south back to Georgia."

"Well, you're a better person than I am," Macy said with a grin. "I would have left town last night. Out of town family be damned!" But Macy knew her friend well; she was always thinking of others.

Macy urged Traveller, Molly's semi-retired old mount, forward with a light squeeze of her legs. Molly was riding Gypsy, the filly she had brought home with her from Kentucky last fall. Now three years old, Gypsy was blossoming into a beautiful young lady. She was already rather tall standing 16.3 hands, but she was as lithe as a cat with long legs that pranced daintily in place as she waited for Traveller to catch up. Her black coat shone brightly in the August sunshine.

"I can't get over how gorgeous Gypsy is. I mean, she's always been a stunner, but wow. Where are you with her training?" Macy asked.

"We're still taking things really slowly. She's only three, so we're not jumping yet except for some
~~~~~

small random logs out on the trail, nothing substantial. Right now I'm just letting her be a horse by taking lots of trail rides, but I'm working on her fitness too. I take her down to our back field and canter along the fence line; she's so good. But with her bowed tendon from last year, we're taking baby steps. She's been completely sound though, so far, so good."

"Excellent! It sounds like you have her in a nice program. As long as you don't overdo anything, which you're not, she shouldn't have a problem with her tendon. Waiting until next year to start jumping will help too."

The girls had a wonderful ride. They rode through the windy trails, crossed a few streams, and had a nice canter through one of the open fields. When they got back to the stable, Beau and his brother, Tate, were waiting for them.

"Y'all certainly look like you had a nice ride," Beau said as he helped Molly down from the saddle. He gave his wife a kiss and then, like any good vet, ran his hand down Gypsy's forelegs, checking for heat. "She's perfect," he said, "just like my wife."

"You two lovebirds are makin' me sick," Tate said, smiling at his little brother. He and Beau had just returned from playing a round of golf. Neither brother was very good, but it was nice to get out on the course every so often.

Molly blushed under the attention. "Let us put the horses away, and then we'll be up for dinner, okay?" Karen was throwing a family BBQ since there were so many friends and family still in town.

"Don't know if I can stand to be away from you that long," Beau said with a teasing tone.

"Oh you," said Macy. "You've got her the rest of your life. Let me have ten more minutes with her." She swatted at him with her crop until both the boys turned

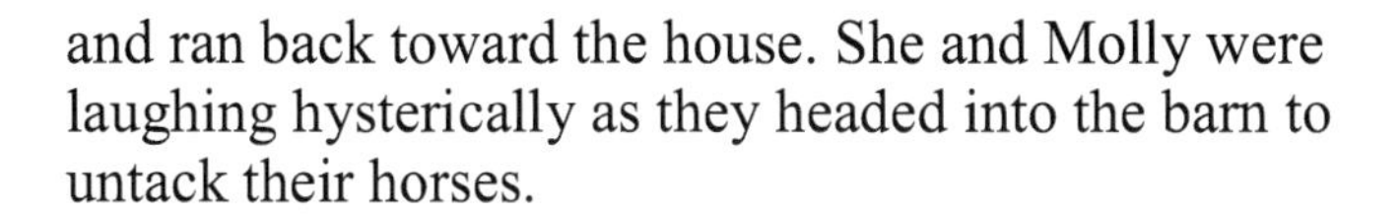

and ran back toward the house. She and Molly were laughing hysterically as they headed into the barn to untack their horses.

~ Chapter 3 ~

"So how was the wedding? I bet Molly was a beautiful bride," stated Cassidy Winters, a fellow intern at Rood and Riddle Hospital in Lexington, Kentucky. She and Macy were on night shift together and, surprisingly, the hospital was quiet.

"She was gorgeous, breathtaking really. Beau couldn't keep his eyes off her," Macy smiled as she remembered the look on his face as Molly walked down the aisle on her father's arm. There wasn't a dry eye in the house. "And the wedding itself was perfect. It was hot, of course, but there were fans in the tent, so it really wasn't that bad."

Cassidy smiled a genuine smile. "I'm glad to hear it. I know I was a monster to both of them last year, but I really am happy for them. Beau's a great guy, and he deserves to be happy."

Macy shrugged. "Well, it's all in the past now. And besides, it didn't stop them from being together, and now they're husband and wife!" Macy still couldn't believe it; her best friend was Mrs. Molly Bridges. She was also happy that, despite the fact that Cassidy had done some serious meddling in Beau's and Molly's relationship, she and Cassidy were finally friends. Cass had apologized to Macy for causing some high school drama, and since then, the two girls had grown closer.

Cassidy's beeper sounded. "Gotta run. But welcome back!" She turned on her heel and disappeared around the corner.

Alone with her thoughts, Macy reflected on the events of the past week. It had felt so good to be home in Maryland; she hadn't realized how much she had missed it until yesterday morning when she packed her bags to leave. She put on a brave face for her mother, but as soon as she got in the car and drove two miles down the road, Macy burst into tears.

That sort of emotional outburst wasn't like her, she acknowledged. She had lived in Kentucky for almost ten years now. Why was she suddenly so homesick? Macy had lived in Lexington without Molly or Beau for almost a year, but maybe their marriage had solidified the fact that they weren't coming back, even though Macy hadn't expected them to.

But now her best friend was married; she was starting a life with the person she'd be with until she was old and grey. Macy had never minded being the single one and found solace in her work and horses, but maybe that wasn't enough anymore. Maybe it was time to focus on meeting someone she could call on her breaks, someone who would be there when she got home to ask about her day. Macy hadn't dated anyone seriously since Dan, the boyfriend she had in vet school.

She and Dan had been together for almost three years before they parted ways. He, too, was in vet school, and the competition between them towards the end had gotten unbearable. When he was offered an internship at the Equine Performance Clinic at Cornell in Ithaca, New York, he jumped at it. "I'd say come with me, but I know you won't," were his parting words.

By then, Macy had been offered her internship at Rood and Riddle, so following him to New York was out of the question. But, she realized, it never crossed his mind to stay in Lexington with her, nor had she suggested they try dating long distance.

Funny, she thought to herself, *I haven't thought about Dan in so long. I must be getting soft in my old age.*

~~~~~

"That's my good boy," Macy praised Hunter after a long gallop through one of the neighboring farm's fields. He bounced along at the walk, eager for more. "If I didn't know better, I'd say you were a spring chicken, not the twenty-something year old man that you are," Macy laughed. She honestly didn't know what she would have done in Kentucky all these years without him, her best friend.

"What would you say," she asked Hunter, "if I told you we might be moving home to Maryland? Would you like that?" Hunter sneezed, and Macy took that as a good sign. "Really? I'd love it too!" She smiled to herself. The thought of packing her bags for good and heading home brought such a sense of relief that she knew it was time to move on. She figured she would join one of the local practices, maybe Beau's, if he'd have her. But in the meantime, she could move back in with her mom. Macy knew it was a little odd to be living at home as a thirty year old, but she knew her mom had plenty of space and would love the company. And her mom still had a barn and fenced fields for Hunter.

Best of all, she'd be right down the street from Molly and Beau. She could swing by Molly's on her lunch break for a quick bite to eat or for a cup of coffee. Yes, it was finally time to return to her Maryland roots.

After Macy cooled out Hunter and put him back in his field, she checked her cell phone. She had a missed call and voicemail from her brother. He sounded upset. "Hey Mace, it's me. Call me the minute you get this."

Macy got a sinking feeling in the pit of her stomach as she hit send and waited for Tommy to pick up.

"Mace?" Tommy answered, his voice cracking.
~~~~~

"Tommy? What's wrong?" Macy could hear Cora sobbing in the background.

"Mace, I'm so sorry, but…mom's gone. She died in a car accident this afternoon." He heard Macy's gasp. "Oh Mace, I'm so sorry to tell you this over the phone," Tommy began crying hysterically.

All Macy could hear was the blood rushing through her ears. "What, Tommy? What did you say? Mom's dead? She can't be dead! I just saw her two days ago! This isn't possible!" She didn't realize that she was screaming at the phone. "I didn't even get to say goodbye!"

"I'm flying out tonight to bring you home. Can you meet me at the airport? We can drive home together."

But Macy didn't hear what her brother was saying. She had fallen to her knees, slamming her hands against the grass. "No!" She cried. "NO!"

~ Chapter 4 ~

Two days later, Macy was sitting alone in the living room in her mom's house when Molly bolted through the front door. As soon as she saw Macy, she ran across the room and the two girls embraced. Molly held her friend tight as a fresh wave of tears began to overtake her.

When Macy was finally able to regain her composure, she looked at her best friend and gave her a watery smile. "You came home early from your honeymoon. You didn't have to do that. I told Erin and your mom not to interrupt your trip."

"That's absurd, Mace. Of course they should have called me. There's nowhere I'd rather be than with you right now." She looked at Macy, tears glistening in both girls' eyes. "I'm so very sorry about your mom. She was such a wonderful person," she said, her voice cracking. "I loved her too. Everyone who knew her did."

The girls dissolved into tears and held each other until Beau came through the front door. After he gave Macy a tight hug, he said, "Now little lady, I've been instructed to bring you over to Molly's parents' for some dinner. Karen said she won't take no for an answer. And Tommy and Cora too, if they're here."

"That's awfully sweet of your mom," Macy said, looking at Molly. "But I really can't be around people right now. And Tommy's still meeting with the funeral director. I should really be here when he gets back."

"Mace, we're not *people*. We're *family*. I'll text Tommy and tell him you're with us and that he can join when he's finished." When Macy looked ready to balk again, Molly hurried on. "And besides, you need to eat. You're skin and bones as it is."

Macy smiled at her two best friends. "I guess I don't have a choice, do I?"

"Nope," said Beau. "I was instructed to carry you out of this house if need be," he said with a smile.

"Okay," relented Macy with a small laugh. "Let's go."

~~~~~

Three days later, Macy was saying goodbye to close friends and other relatives who had come for the wake. Held at Karen's house after the funeral, Macy was touched that so many people had showed up to honor her mother.

"Hadley was one of the kindest, most selfless people I ever met," said Evelyn, a neighbor. "I know you're headed back to Kentucky after this, but, please, know that I'm here for you, Macy. Call any time."

Karen and Molly tried to shoo Macy away when she tried to help clean up after the last person had left, but she insisted. "Please, you've all been so wonderful to me. Let me help – let me keep busy."

The past few days since finding out about Hadley's death had been a terrible whirlwind, a nightmare. Everything Macy had known about life, everything she was sure of, was gone. Her mother's unconditional love, support, encouragement, it was all gone. Some reckless drunk driver had ended everything, changing Macy's entire life, in the blink of an eye. For what felt like the hundredth time that day, tears started to well up in her eyes, but she tried not to cry, and she tried not to let the guilt overtake her. Since Tommy's call, all Macy could think about was all the time she had missed with her mom by living in Kentucky. If only she had gone to vet school closer to home, she could have had
~~~~~

more time with her mom, more memories, more of everything.

Later that night back at the family house, Tommy, Cora, and Macy sat at the dining room table, mugs of hot tea steaming in their hands. It had been a long, emotionally-exhausting day, and they were relieved it was over.

They rehashed the details of the day, recounting all the memories that were shared with them by friends and acquaintances of their mother. There had been so many; they had had no idea that their mother had touched so many people's lives.

"Every single person told me how mom had gone on and on about her daughter, the vet," Tommy said with a wink. "I guess her son, the accountant, isn't quite so exciting," he laughed.

"Well you know horse people," smiled Cora. "They have a one-track mind! And all the hunt club members told me that even though your mom didn't ride with them anymore, she was still active with the club's social events and whatnot. It made me happy that she had so many friends and such a full calendar."

"I know," agreed Tommy. "We don't even live that far away, and I was still surprised to hear how active she was in the community – she certainly kept busy."

The three talked and laughed and cried way into the night. When Tommy and Cora got up to leave, Tommy promised that he'd be back early the next day to start going over their mother's affairs. And then the reading of the will would take place the following week. Macy had taken a temporary leave of absence from the hospital but told her supervisor she figured she'd be gone probably around a month. There was so much to take care of.

Even though it was after one in the morning and

she was truly exhausted, Macy also felt a little wired. Being overtired always did that to her, kept her brain going when she wished she could turn it off and go to sleep.

Instead of curling up in bed in her childhood room, she wandered the big, empty house, room by room. In the family room, she remembered how her mom would put the Christmas tree in the center of the bay windows, and how the family had gathered around it, bright and early each year. The best Christmases had been the ones before her father had passed.

The kitchen, her favorite room in the house, was big, warm, and inviting with its built-in alcove seating and its fireplace on the opposite wall. Even though there was another fireplace in the living room, they had always hung their Christmas stockings over this one, claiming it was easier for Santa to come through the kitchen so that he could grab his milk and cookies on his way in, conveniently laid out on the counter.

Macy wandered into the library where the shelves were crammed with dozens of books and the walls were lined with family photos. Her mother had been a voracious reader, and had countless mysteries, memoirs, and fiction novels. The framed pictures on the walls depicted their happy life: Tommy, clad in his cap and gown on the day of his high school graduation; Macy, saluting a judge after her first test at Devon; their entire family smiling broadly in front of the Grand Canyon.

She sat in her mom's favorite reading chair, a red tartan-patterned chair tucked into the back corner of the room. Next to the chair was a small end table with a book lying on top. Its marker showed that her mother had been halfway through. With trembling hands, Macy picked up the book and held it to her chest, close to her heart. This might have been one of the last things her mother had touched on this earth. She looked at the well-worn cover, *The Great Gatsy*, her mom's favorite. She must have read it a million times.

Macy held the book tightly and let her overwhelming tears of sadness take her away.

~ Chapter 5 ~

The next couple of days after the funeral were still pretty busy. Lots of friends and neighbors stopped by to check on Macy, even though they had just seen her at the funeral and wake. Hearty casseroles and freshly baked pies and cakes were piled high on the kitchen counters and in the refrigerator. Macy had so much food that she invited Molly and Beau to come dine with her one night.

"How've you been holdin' up, Mace?" Beau asked in between large bites of lasagna. Molly had been stopping by regularly, but Beau had gotten back to work. He and Molly had decided they'd take another belated honeymoon later in the year, or early next. Being home with Macy was most important.

"I've been okay. Honestly, I've had so many visitors and calls, texts and emails that I really haven't had much time to be alone with my thoughts. I guess that's a good thing though," she replied with a half-smile. Macy sounded better than she looked. Her eyes were red-rimmed and sad, and she looked like she had lost a few pounds. Very skinny to begin with, Macy couldn't afford to lose any weight.

"Have you decided what you'd like to do with your mom's things? Would you like to donate her clothes? Or would you just like to leave everything alone for now?" Molly asked, unsure of which direction Macy's grief would take her. After Molly's grandmom had passed away, Karen went to work immediately cleaning out her mother's house, donating clothing and other items. But she remembered how her Aunt Linda, Karen's sister, hadn't wanted any part in emptying the house. She felt it was too soon and didn't want to let go of all of the memories just yet.

Macy sighed as she reached for the bottle of red wine. She poured herself a healthy serving and then passed it to Beau. “Don’t worry,” she said as she noticed Molly’s concerned glance, “this is the first bit of alcohol I’ve had in weeks.” When Molly smiled, she continued. “I think it’s best if I start going through everything now. We have the reading of the will next week, but in the meantime, I can at least go through mom’s clothes. She had a lot of nice things that I’d like to donate. It makes me happy to think that someone else, someone who really needs them, will give them a second home.”

“I agree,” Molly said. “And I’m here to help. Let me know what you need. If you’d like a second pair of hands, I’m on it. If you’d rather go through her things yourself, that’s fine too.”

Macy reached across the table and took Molly’s hand. “Thank you. You have been such a wonderful friend.” She reached out for Beau’s hand too. “You too, Beau. I don’t know what I would have done without you both. I still can’t believe you came home early from your honeymoon for me. I love you guys.”

~~~~~

Macy sat in silence after the reading of her mom’s will. Next to her was Tommy, and then Cora sat to his right. Neither sibling had had any real of idea of their mother’s financial situation; they only knew that their mom had been comfortable. But now they realized that their mother had been extremely comfortable thanks to some wise investments.

Hadley had left the family farm to Macy – the large house, barn, and forty acres all belonged to her. To Tommy and Cora, she had left all of her stocks and bonds
~~~~~

with all investments totaling just over one million dollars, which was approximately what Macy could get for the farm should she decide to sell. *I can't believe this is really happening*, she thought. *Mom is really gone.*

As they walked out of the attorney's office, Macy begged off lunch. "If it's okay, I'd like to just go home. This day," she paused, tears threatening to spill over. "This had been quite a day already." It wasn't even noon yet.

"I understand," Tommy said as he pulled his sister in for an embrace. "Call me if you want to talk. We can come over later too, if you'd like some company for dinner."

Macy nodded as Cora came over to hug her as well. "I'll call you guys later. Dinner sounds like a good idea – I still have some casseroles in the freezer."

When she returned to the farm and pulled up in front of the house, she looked at her home with fresh eyes. *This all belongs to me*, she thought, weeping again as she got out of the car. She loved this house more than any other place in the world, but she didn't want it like this. Not with her mother gone. Should she keep it? Would it feel like *home* without her mother's presence? Could she make a life for herself here?

Macy spent the rest of the afternoon by herself, alone in her mother's room. She and Molly had already cleaned out most of the closet and dresser drawers. Macy was happy to be donating multiple bags to the local women's shelter. She was holding onto a few items, things that he been her mother's favorites like her mint green cashmere sweater, her riding habit, and her fuzzy bathrobe with playful foxes printed on it.

As Macy sat on the bed and looked around the room, she marveled how her mother had decorated so tastefully. Typically, bedrooms tended to be overlooked as very few people but the owners saw them. But Hadley had left no stone unturned. The high white coffered ceilings added beautiful texture and matched the wainscoting that circled the perimeter. The room had been painted a sage green and a variety of foxhunting prints adorned the walls. An antique riding crop had been hung above the doorway to the master bath.

Over the bed hung a portrait that Hadley had commissioned of the four of them on horseback. Hadley was riding her old foxhunter, Chase; her father sat proudly on his horse, Roman. She and Tommy sat astride their fat ponies, Crimson and Foxy. The picture had been taken about a year before her father had died. Shortly thereafter, her mother had the painting commissioned, and it had become one of her most cherished possessions.

Later that evening after dinner, Macy, Tommy, and Cora sat in the living room drinking coffee.

"So," Tommy said, breaking the silence. "This has been quite a day, hasn't it?" Both of the girls nodded in agreement. "What are you going to do about the farm? Do you want to keep it? Will you move home from Kentucky?"

"Well, I still need to think on it some more, but my gut says to keep it. It's our home, you know? And even though it doesn't really feel like home without mom in it, it will one day. I don't think I could bear to part with it. It's all we have left of her, and I think she'd want it to stay in the family." Macy swallowed the lump in her throat and continued. "I think I'll head back to Kentucky, finish out my internship, and then come home. For good. My internship is up in December, so just a few more months."

Tommy and Cora both exchanged glances and smiled at each other. "I'm so glad to hear it," said Tommy. "Because I wouldn't want my child's aunt to be so far away." He grinned like a cat who ate the canary.

"What?" Macy cried, jumping to her feet. "You're pregnant?" She ran over to Cora, who was beaming.

"Yes," Cora said, jumping up to hug Macy. "But don't tell anyone. I literally found out this morning, so it's very early."

Tommy joined them in their hug, but soon their smiles faded. "Mom would have been overjoyed to have a grandchild," Macy said, tears glistening. "But I am so happy for you two – I can't wait to be an aunt."

~~~~~

Macy was almost finished packing her bags when the doorbell rang. She was leaving for Lexington first thing in morning. She peered out her window and saw a man standing on her front porch. He was tall, easily over six foot, and his salt-and-peppered grey hair told her that he was probably in his forties.

When I move back for good, she thought, *I'm getting a dog*. She didn't like the idea of living alone in this big house in the country without the protection of a dog.

"Hi, can I help you?" Macy asked as she opened the door.

The man gave her a small smile and offered his hand. His face was very tan, and he was dressed in jeans, work boots, and a well-worn polo shirt. "Hi, my name's Adam Cleary. I bought the farm next door a few months back."

Macy remembered her mother telling her about her new neighbor. Nice, but somewhat standoffish, is what Hadley had said about the man who had bought the old Radnor place, as it was known to the locals.

"That's right, I remember my mother telling me.
~~~~~

I'm Macy Holland. Nice to meet you," she said, shaking his hand. "What can I do for you?"

"Well, first I wanted to offer my condolences about your mom. I had only spoken with her a few times, but she was a very nice lady. I knew she was going to be a great neighbor."

"Thank you, I appreciate your kind words about her."

"Of course," Adam said, clearing his throat. "I know this is a hard time, and please forgive me if I'm overstepping, but I wanted to inquire about this farm. If you're going to sell it, I'd like first right of refusal."

Macy was taken aback. Had he really come over to ask her for the farm? She was shocked that someone she'd never met had the nerve to come over less than a month after her mother's death and ask to buy her place, her home.

When Macy didn't respond, Adam continued. "I don't know if your mom told you, but I'm a racehorse trainer, and I was hoping to expand my farm. I only have twenty acres, so I'd like to have more so I can keep the weanlings here before they go to the track, and then I'd also bring some horses in for lay-ups and whatnot. Anyway, like I said, no rush, I was just hoping to have first option should you decide to put this place on the market."

After he finished, Macy exploded. "The nerve of you! My mother is barely cold in her grave, and you have the audacity to come over here now, less than a month after she's been ripped away from me, hoping to buy my land! You've got to be kidding me. Please tell me this is some sick joke."

Adam's face grew redder as Macy unleashed her fury on him. Then he exploded back. "You wait just one minute," he spat. "I came over here to meet you and tell you how sorry I am about your mother. I don't care if you sell or not, but if you do, I figured I'd do you a favor and make it easy on you. You wouldn't have to go through the trouble of listing the farm. I was going to take it as-is."

"Oh you're doing me a favor? Is that what this is? I think it looks more like an opportunist shark circling his prey at their weakest moment. Maybe you thought that I wouldn't be thinking clearly, so you could get this place for a song. I think that's what this is about!"

Adam shook his head. "You've got it all wrong. The last thing I'd do is try and take advantage of someone. I merely wanted to let you know that if you decided to sell, I'm interested. That's all." He couldn't believe that Macy had twisted his intentions around, but he shouldn't have been too surprised. She was grieving, and her mother's death had been so sudden.

"Well guess what, neighbor? This farm isn't for sale, ever, *especially* to you!" And with that, Macy slammed the door in his face.

Adam turned and walked off the porch, and then made a right, heading across the front yard back to his farm. This had been a mistake. His assistant had told him to tread lightly if he was going to make this offer, but he really didn't think he'd come across that offensively. Houses are sold all the time after someone dies – that's just how life works. The last thing he'd wanted to do was upset Macy, but he thought there'd be no harm in putting the bug in her ear that he was interested in her place.

But what he hadn't considered was that his new neighbor was a feisty one. Clearly, he had touched a nerve about her home because he could see that she'd wanted to claw his eyes out. *Fine, then. Keep the place. I hope that's the last I'll see of her any time soon*, he thought drily.

~ Chapter 6 ~

"So the drive back was okay? I told you I would have driven with you and then flown back." Molly said over the phone when Macy called to let her know she'd arrived safely in Lexington.

"I know, and I appreciated the offer, but it was nice to be alone, do some thinking. Besides, I'm still kind of fuming over the run-in I had with my delightful new neighbor yesterday," Macy said sarcastically.

"Uh oh," Molly sighed. "What happened?"

Macy told her how Adam had come knocking, asking what her plans were with her mother's farm. "I probably shouldn't have, but I exploded on him. I couldn't believe it. Who does that? Who comes over so soon after a funeral and asks to purchase the property? Doesn't that seem a little low to you?"

"Yeah," Molly admitted. "A little. But I can see where he's coming from too. He's the neighbor, and he wants the property for his horses. I think he should have waited a little longer, or even wrote you a quick note, but I don't think he meant to upset you."

Macy sighed. "I guess not. But it was his tone. I don't know, it's hard to pinpoint exactly, but he just came across like a pompous jerk. After I yelled at him, he actually yelled back!"

"Okay, that's definitely not cool. That's no way to treat someone who's just lost a parent. That's actually no way to treat anyone, period."

"Right?" Macy agreed. "I know that deep down he probably meant no harm, and I know I was being oversensitive because mom is gone and the farm is mine now, but, I kind of hate him a little!"

Molly laughed. "Most people have a neighbor or

two they hate – it's totally normal! Hopefully he'll keep to himself. You two are separated by enough space that you really shouldn't run across him much."

"Very true. I hope I never see his arrogant face again."

~~~~~

Lexington in late September is exquisite. The weather is dry, the air crisp, but with the sun shining, it was often warm too. Macy had been back in Kentucky for about a week, and while it was comforting to get back into the normal routine of her life, she was anxious to get home to Maryland. She thought about ending her internship early, but decided against it after speaking with her supervisor, Roy. He told her she should do what was best for her, but she felt a loyalty to him and the hospital.

She hoped that the next few months would fly by and that when she returned home in December, it would be with the knowledge that she'd never leave again. It was time to return to Maryland for good.

In between her shifts at the hospital, Macy kept as busy as possible and started packing up her apartment. After ten years in the bluegrass state, she had accumulated more than she had originally thought. Since she was moving back to a completely furnished house, she decided to give most of her belongings away but also sold some things on ebay and craigslist. And while it was sad to see the rooms around her become sparse and bare, she felt relief at the thought of closing this chapter for good.

On Monday, the hospital was hopping. Macy, coffee in hand, walked down the hall with her charts, poking her head in and out of stalls, checking on her patients. Everyone was just as they should be.
~~~~~

"Dr. Holland," a voice called from behind her.

Macy turned and saw William Berkley, the owner and trainer of one of her current patients, a dappled grey thoroughbred gelding named Fitz.

"Hi, Mr. Berkley. Have you come to check on Fitz?"

The horse was in for two minor issues, a suspensory injury and a bowed tendon. Neither were too serious or life-threatening, but at five years of age, they were most likely career-ending for this racehorse.

"I have. I actually wanted to speak with you and Dr. Jackson, if he's around."

"I believe he's in his office. Follow me, and let's see if we can catch him."

As the two walked through the halls to Roy Jackson's office, Macy noticed that Mr. Berkley seemed uncomfortable as he was fidgeting with the keys in his pocket. She could hear him jingling them around as he moved alongside her.

Roy was seated at his desk reading a file on his computer. He looked up and smiled as the two entered.

"Mr. Berkley," Roy said as he rose, walked around his desk, and extended his hand. "It's good to see you." The two men shook hands. "Have a seat, won't you?"

All three sat down at a small table situated in the corner of Roy's office. Mr. Berkley cleared his throat and began.

"When I was here last week, I was told that Fitz's prognosis for a full recovery was good, but that it would take several months. Do you still believe that to be the case?"

Macy spoke up. "Yes, that's true. The combo suspensory injury and bowed tendon will put Fitz out of commission and on stall rest for four to six months. Of course, he can do the majority of that recovery at home. If you're prepared to move him back, we can discharge him as early as tomorrow."

Mr. Berkley nodded. "Yes, I understand that he could recuperate at home, but that's the problem. Unfortunately, Fitz is five, so this was most likely going to be his last year racing. And also unfortunately, he's a gelding, so there's no chance of him having a stud career. I've been thinking it over these past few days and, while I hate to do it, I've decided to have him put down."

Macy gasped and looked over at Roy, who also appeared to be a little shocked. "Mr. Berkley," Roy said, "I understand that racing is a business and that once a horse is unable to earn his keep, he needs to move on. But, like Macy said, Fitz is slated to make a full recovery after a few months of stall rest. Perhaps you could allow him to recuperate and then try and rehome him through a retired racehorse placement organization. As long as he makes a full recovery, he could have a very successful second career."

"I'm sorry, but I just can't do that. I don't have the space, nor the time for him to recover. He needs to go, now."

Macy's blood was boiling. She could feel the heat rising in her cheeks, but she tried to remain calm. She'd lived and worked in this area long enough to understand how the racing industry operated, but never had she seen an owner give up on a horse without even trying to give him a chance. Fitz had been admitted to the hospital just prior to Macy returning to Lexington, and he was an incredible horse. Not only had he won thousands at the track, he had a heart of gold. The staff had nicknamed him "the love bug" because he was so friendly.

"Mr. Berkley," Macy said. "How about I make some calls and see what I can do. I have a few contacts at

CANTER and New Vocations. I'm sure someone around here has the room for him to recover and can then place him shortly thereafter."

"I'm sorry, but like I said, I don't have the time. Finances have been very tight; I've been walking on thin ice for months now. I need to have him put down. Immediately."

"No!" Macy exclaimed, quickly rising to her feet. "I won't allow it."

"Excuse me?" Mr. Berkley asked, also rising to his feet. "I am his owner, and I have final say!"

"Macy!" Roy said sharply, looking at his intern. "Mr. Berkley, I apologize for her outburst. If you'd both please take a seat, I'm sure we can come to a conclusion that works for everyone, Fitz included."

"I've made up my mind," said Mr. Berkley. "I can't worry about him any longer. Put him down, today!"

"No!" Shouted Macy again. "I will not stand by and watch a perfectly good horse be put to death." Macy's hands were balled into fists and she had started to cry. "No more unnecessary death will occur on my watch. I'll take him, Mr. Berkley. I'll assume full ownership of him immediately. Sign the papers and walk out of here. Fitz will be my responsibility."

"Macy, calm down," said Roy, walking over to her side. He knew that she had been under an incredible amount of stress since her mother's passing. This was not typical behavior for her. "I understand your concern for the horse, but it is against the hospital's rules for you to assume ownership of a horse that's currently under our care."

"Yes, I know," Macy said, looking Roy directly in the eye, tears streaming down her face. "Then as of this moment, I am no longer a member of the staff here." Then she turned back to Mr. Berkley and extended her hand. “Do we have a deal?”

Mr. Berkley hesitated for a moment but then shook Macy’s hand. “Deal. The horse is yours.”

~ Chapter 7 ~

"Hey! Perfect timing – I was just about to give you a call to check in." Molly exclaimed. "How's Kentucky?" It had been a few days since the two had a chance to catch up.

"Oh, it's great," Macy said sarcastically. "So, I did a thing today. Do you remember the name of the company you used to ship Gypsy back east?"

"Uh oh. That doesn't sound good. What's up?"

Macy was close to tears as she told Molly what had happened at the hospital earlier in the day. She was heartbroken that she had quit on the spot, putting Roy in a tough position, but she didn't know what else to do. She wasn't going to let Fitz die. She'd never be able to live with herself if she had turned her back on him.

"There's absolutely nothing wrong with this horse," she told Molly. "He just needs some time to heal, and then he'll be as good as new. He could be adopted anywhere for almost any discipline, but his owner was being hardheaded. I've seen it happen before where they get so worried about finances that they start making rash decisions, but I've never seen it go down like this. He was adamant that Fitz had to die. I had to do it. I had to save him."

"You made the right decision, Mace, don't give it a second thought. I think any of us would have done the same thing. Was Roy upset at you?" Molly knew from Beau that Roy was a wonderful boss, but this sounded like it had been a precarious situation.

"Yeah he was upset. He kept saying that had I not exploded, he was sure he could have calmed the owner down and made a smart decision for everyone. But I don't know if that's true." Macy sighed loudly. "Roy did say that he knows I've been under pressure though, so I think he was somewhat sympathetic."

Macy continued to tell Molly that she had packed her belongings and then met Barb, the owner of the stable where Hunter was boarded, at the hospital where she had arrived to trailer Fitz back to her place. Macy settled him in the barn there in the stall next to Hunter. She had told the boys to play nice because they were brothers now.

"So, what's the plan now? When will you be home?" Molly was upset that Macy had had such a terrible day, but she was overjoyed that her friend would be home sooner than later.

"I need to call the shipping company and schedule that, and then I need to finish packing. I've been gradually throwing junk out or selling things on craigslist, but I still think I might need to rent a U-Haul. I'm going to call Tommy and see if he can fly out here and then drive back with me. Maybe he can drive the U-Haul, and I'll drive my car."

"Let me know what you'd like me to do. If Tommy can't drive you home, I definitely can. Just let me know what you need."

~~~~~

Macy woke early the following day and walked into the kitchen to make some coffee. She had lived in this apartment for the past five years, moving in just after she had started vet school; it was going to be hard to say goodbye. Moving boxes were everywhere, but she took a few minutes to sit by herself and think about everything that had just happened. Was she really unemployed? What would she do now?

Tommy would be arriving the next day, and the two would load up the U-Haul and head east together.
~~~~~

Macy was so thankful that her brother was able to help her and see her through this tough time in her life. Every time she thought she was doing okay, she'd do or think of something she wanted to call and tell her mom about. And then she'd be reminded, for what felt like the thousandth time, that her mom was gone.

Macy had always been a planner, so she did what she did best, she made a list. It consisted of short and long-term goals and objectives. In the near future, she told herself she'd concentrate on moving home, unpacking herself, and settling in her horses. *Horses!* She thought. *I have two now.* This was going to be another change, but one that she was actually ready for. She was always ready to save a life, and Fitz deserved a happy ending.

After everyone was settled into their new Maryland lives, Macy would look for another job. That was the only item listed under the "long term" column. Beau had started his own practice where he made farm calls. She knew that he was doing well and picking up new clients every day. Maybe she could be his assistant until she found something more permanent. Even if he could just give her some part-time work, she'd be happy. Macy had always been pretty frugal, so she had quite a nice savings built up that she could live off of until she got back on her feet. She realized that she could also make some extra income by boarding some horses at her farm.

Satisfied that she had a plan, Macy grabbed another box, some packing tape, a black magic marker, and headed into her bedroom. She had less than twenty-four hours to pack up her life in Kentucky, for good.

~~~~~
~~~~~

"At last. We made it!" Cried Macy as she and her brother parked their vehicles in her driveway and got out. "Home never looked so good." They were back in Maryland, and it had been a long trip.

Tommy arrived in Lexington early that morning, and after Macy met him at the airport, they packed up the U-Haul and Macy's old Audi A6 and headed east. Macy was glad that she was following behind her brother and had the car to herself. As soon as she pulled the door shut to her apartment and dropped the key off to the landlord, she started feeling emotional. But by the time she was driving past familiar sights for the last time for who knew how long, she was all out sobbing.

But now that she was home, she realized that what she was feeling was an intense sense of relief. She was no longer alone. Molly and Beau and Molly's parents were a few miles up the street, and Tommy and Cora were also just a short car ride away. And best of all, Hunter and Fitz were scheduled to arrive tomorrow and would be right outside her back door. She could visit with them any time, day or night.

"Do you want to start unpacking?" Tommy asked.

"Oh my goodness, no way. It's almost midnight. Go home to Cora. I'm going to go to bed myself and will tackle all this tomorrow." Macy went over and hugged her brother tight. "Thank you so much, for everything. I don't know what I'd do without you."

"You are more than welcome, sis. I'm just so happy to have you home. Cora and I will come over tomorrow and help you get all this under control."

When Macy unlocked the door and walked inside, she felt at peace. She would make this house a home again, she promised herself. *The first thing I'm doing after I unpack and get this house in order*, she thought, *is head to the Humane Society for a dog*.

~ Chapter 8 ~

October blew in cool and crisp, typical of autumn in Maryland. The trees were in their full glory displaying an array of brilliant red, orange, and yellow leaves in the late afternoon sun. Macy smiled to herself as she returned home from a trail ride on Hunter.

Trotting alongside the big horse was Mint Julep, the Jack Russell Terrier mix Macy rescued from the local shelter. The moment she saw the dog in the cage, wagging her little tail like crazy and barking at Macy, she knew she'd found her dog. She named her Mint Julep to help keep her Kentucky memories fresh. Julep was white with brown spots; Macy especially loved the spot surrounding her right eye, just like an eyepatch, giving the dog a pirate-like appearance.

Hunter and Fitz made the trek east without any problems and settled easily into farm life. Fitz was on stall rest for at least four months, but Hunter was content to go out into the fields by himself. Macy kept him in the fields to the right side of the barn so Fitz could always see his friend by looking out the back window of his stall. The two enjoyed each other's company, but neither seemed too herd-bound, thankfully.

As they approached the stable yard, Macy noticed a man leaning against the fence by the barn. *Who could that be?* She wondered.

Julep ran ahead, barking at the stranger, so Macy urged Hunter into a trot to quickly cover the ground in between. By the time she got close, Julep was lying on her back, and kicking her leg as the stranger scratched her stomach. *Some guard dog*.

But then Macy realized that this man was no stranger. It was her neighbor, Adam Cleary. The last person she wanted to see.

After he finished petting Julep, Adam looked up and smiled. "I'm sure I'm the last person you want to see, but I wanted to come over and apologize for my behavior the first time we met. It was insensitive of me to approach you so soon after your mother's passing."

Macy dismounted and pulled the reins over Hunter's head. Adam went around to the right side of the horse, rolled up her stirrup, and loosened the girth a notch. Macy smiled at him as she did the same on the left side.

"I appreciate the apology, Mr. Cleary. And I'm sorry for my outburst as well. As you can imagine, it's been a very stressful time."

"Adam," he said matter-of-factly. "Call me Adam."

Adam came around and placed a hand on Hunter's neck. Then he ran it over his shoulder and down his leg. Macy watched him curiously.

"Sorry," he said when he straightened up. "Habit. I don't know if you remember, but I'm a racehorse trainer. I'm always checking out legs, feeling for heat."

Macy smiled. "I remember. And I'm a horse vet. I don't believe I told you that during our last…encounter."

Adam smiled again. Macy noticed that his eyes were ice blue, which complemented his tanned, somewhat lined face. She would have guessed that Adam was in his early forties, but it was always hard to tell with horse people who were outside, in all kinds of weather, day in and day out. He had a rugged feel to him, but he was far from a cowboy. And while he smiled a little, it was hard to get a true read on him. She could tell that he wanted to befriend her, but he also had an aloof, almost mysterious manner that she couldn't quite trust.

"No, you didn't tell me, but I heard. Word is

through the grapevine is that you're back from Kentucky for good."

"I am," Macy said. "And what grapevine are you getting your information from, if you don't mind my asking?"

"Oh, just neighbors and clients and the like. One of my clients is a foxhunter who knew your mother, so I did a little research on my new neighbor," he said casually with a sly smile.

"Research?"

"Yeah, remember I had wanted to purchase your farm. It was my client who had told me your mom had passed, so that's when I decided to ask you about it. That same client is the one who told me you had returned."

"Forgive me for saying so, Adam, but that's kind of sneaky."

"Are you telling me that you've never wondered about the people you live near? That, if the opportunity arose, you wouldn't do a little investigating?"

"If I was curious about my neighbors, I would walk over and personally get to know them. That's how we are around here. We're friendly. We don't hide behind clients and computer screens. And we don't listen to *the word through the grapevine*." Macy didn't mean to come across so rude, but this man irked her. In every way he bothered her. Overall, he seemed nice enough, and she was pleasantly surprised that he had come over to smooth things out after their previous mishap, but it was like he knew the wrong thing to say, but still said it anyway.

"Now Macy, I think we're getting off on the wrong foot again. I didn't mean any harm. I'm not as *friendly* as you all are. I'm from up north where people tend to keep to themselves a bit. I'm not one to come around often, asking questions, and getting in everyone's way."

"So then why are you here?"

Adam sighed and looked out over the fields. "I'm not sure," he answered. "I felt bad about how I acted during our first meeting, and I wanted to make it right between us since we're neighbors. But I can see that I wasted my time," he said, temper beginning to flare. *Why did this one always try to start a fight?*

"You did," Macy retorted. "Have a nice day, Mr. Cleary." She stared at him coolly in the eye. Adam held that contact for longer than he should, making her uncomfortable. Before he turned and walked off though, she could have sworn she saw his eyes soften a bit.

~~~~~

"Molly, I swear, that man is incredulous." Macy spat over the phone later that evening. "I truly believe that he deliberately says whatever he can just to get a rise out of me. Why else would he have told me that he did a little *research* on me?"

Molly couldn't hold back her laughter. "He was probably just making conversation. Maybe he was just trying to joke around with you. Or maybe he likes you, Mace! Have you considered that?"

That was the last conclusion Macy would have come to. She laughed. "I'm pretty sure that's not it. I have to say though, I am a little upset at myself for snapping at him again. Even though he clearly knows how to push my buttons, I'm usually so much better at keeping my cool and remaining professional. I don't know what's wrong with me lately."

"Mace, you lost your mother. You quit your job. You moved back home after almost ten years away. You've been under a tremendous amount of stress since Hadley died in August. You need to cut yourself some
~~~~~

slack. It's okay to kind of be all over the place right now."

"I know, and thanks for saying that. But I don't want to be all over the place. I just want to be me again. I feel like," she paused for a moment, gathering her thoughts, "like I'm on the brink of something. Like I'm teetering on the edge of insanity. On one side, I'm me, I'm Macy, and I'm fine. And on the other, I'm quitting jobs, rescuing horses, and fighting with neighbors. I don't even recognize that girl, but what's worse is that I don't know how to control her."

"I promise you, Mace, all this is absolutely normal given the circumstances. You just need time. With each passing day you'll feel better and better until you're firmly back on solid ground again. It might take months, even a year, so cut yourself some slack."

Macy sure hoped so because she wasn't used to feeling out of control. And she wasn't used to being so sensitive. She didn't know why she wanted to pick a fight with Adam. He had come over today to apologize, and she had stood there, waiting for him to falter so she could pounce. And now that she thought about it, she and Adam did have a nice moment before she spoiled it. She liked the way he had run his hands down Hunter's legs, checking for any heat.

However, it had bothered her that he had done some *research* on her and the farm. Why couldn't he have just come over and introduced himself like a typical neighbor? Macy didn't know why, but she felt like there was more than meets the eye where Adam Cleary was concerned. And while she'd like to get to know him a little better, as a neighbor, she figured it was better for both of them if she just steered clear. *We are like oil and vinegar*, Macy thought drily.

~ Chapter 9 ~

It was the last Saturday in October, but the temperatures had soared to seventy degrees. Macy and Erin, wanting to take advantage of this Indian Summer, were at the Sorrensons' farm, watching Molly work Gypsy in the outdoor ring.

Macy and Erin sat on the top rail of the fence while Molly trotted around, doing lateral work down the long side.

"She's looking great," Erin called to her sister. "Nice and supple."

After she warmed up the filly, Macy set up some poles on the ground, known as cavaletti, so Molly could officially start her jump training with Gypsy. After Gypsy had mastered trotting and cantering over the poles on the ground, shortening and lengthening her stride as asked, then they'd start jumping small crossrails.

"My goal is to get her jumping a very small course of crossrails over the winter," Molly said breathlessly as Gypsy breezed through the cavaletti perfectly on her first try.

"With the way she's been going, I'd say that will be an easy goal to accomplish," Macy laughed. Gypsy was such a willing horse and tried her hardest for Molly. They were a special pair.

Macy walked back over to the fence and leaned against it next to Erin. "I'm glad you made it out here today," Macy said, looking up at Erin. "It's too nice of a day to be stuck in the house."

Erin gave a small laugh. "Trust me, with the way Kevin's been acting these days, I couldn't get out of the house fast enough."

Macy was surprised to hear this. Erin and Kevin

always seemed to have a wonderful relationship. She turned to Erin, concerned for her friend, and asked, "What's going on? Are you guys okay?"

"That's a good question, and I'm not sure how to answer it." Erin shook her head. "It all started when I told him earlier this year that I was thinking of getting another horse, something young like Gypsy, so I could have a fun, new project, and he just flipped out on me. He said that instead of spending my extra time running up here taking care of a horse, we should be settling down and starting a family."

"Oh goodness. I'm sorry, Erin, I had no idea you guys had been fighting, but I had wondered why you hadn't gotten another horse yet."

"That's why. He pitched such a fit about it that I just haven't had it in me to get another." She sighed. "The truth is, I'm not ready to have a baby yet, and he said if I couldn't give him a child, then it wasn't fair for me to get another horse."

Macy couldn't believe that. "He honestly said that?"

"He did. And I can't believe that I actually listened. But I feel bad too. I had always intended to have a family, and before we got married, we were both on the same page about wanting kids someday. But that was so long ago that it was easy to imagine that one day I'd get there, that I'd be ready for them. And I know that I'm thirty-three and the clock's ticking, but I'm nowhere near ready to become a mother."

Macy climbed on the fence and put her arm around her friend. "It's okay not to be ready yet. And you know, what? It's okay to decide that you're never going to be ready. We can't see into the future and know exactly how we're going to feel about something years down the road. I definitely don't think you should have kids until you are completely sure the time is right for you. In the meantime, have you two thought about seeing a marriage counselor? Because it's not fair of Kevin to pressure you like this."

Erin shook her head. "We haven't looked into seeing anyone yet, but I think we're just about there. Things at home have been pretty miserable," she said, wiping a stray tear from her cheek.

"Does Molly know about this?" Macy asked.

Erin nodded. "Yes, Molly knows what's going on, but I haven't mentioned anything to my parents. I haven't wanted them to worry. I guess I just keep hoping that one day I'll wake up and magically be ready and want kids. But the older I get and the more we fight about it, the more I'm starting to think that it's just not for me. That I'm just not meant to be a mother."

"And you know what? That's *okay*. If you decide that kids aren't for you, that's more than okay. I'm sure you and Kevin will get through it, but I definitely think you should talk to someone. A marriage counselor could only help."

The two girls hopped down from the fence and embraced. "Thank you for listening. I'm sorry to be troubling you after all you've gone through this fall."

Macy hugged her friend back and said, "Don't apologize. No matter what's happened recently, I'm always here for you. If you ever want to talk, or just get out of the house for a bit, please call me. I get a little lonely at home."

At that moment, Molly rode over, finished with her work out on Gypsy. She took one look at Erin's sad face and knew exactly what the two girls had been talking about. Her heart ached for her sister, but she knew that Erin and Kevin would work through this rough patch. They loved each other too much not to make things right.

~~~~~

Back at her house that evening, Macy was humming to herself as she cleaned up her kitchen after dinner. She realized that she was actually happy. While her heart had broken for poor Erin and what she was going through, Macy had really enjoyed being with two of her favorite people.

After watching Molly ride, the three girls sat outside on the porch and drank tall glasses of iced tea that Karen had prepared for them. They couldn't believe that they were enjoying a cold beverage outside so late in October. Typically, they would have warmed up inside the house, next to a roaring fire in the fireplace, clutching large mugs of coffee or hot chocolate. Maryland weather could be pretty inconsistent.

"Mind if I join you girls?" Karen asked, walking outside with her own glass of tea.

"Of course not," Macy said. "Please do!"

"So, Macy," Karen said, "how do you like working with Beau?"

About two weeks ago, Macy had started working part-time with Beau's practice. He was hoping he could afford to bring her on full-time eventually, but he would need to build up his client base a little more before that could happen.

"I love it – it's just like old times!" Macy laughed. "It's so different from what we're used to in the hospital since neither of us have ever made farm calls before. It's nice because now we're dealing with more minor things, like cuts and scrapes and vaccinations. Our days are much less traumatic, and I don't know about Beau, but I've been embracing the relative ease of it."

"Do you two work together, or do you go your
~~~~~

separate ways during the day?" Erin asked.

"Both. Typically, how it's been working so far is that Beau gives me a call in the morning and tells me where I'm needed. Sometimes we go our separate ways giving vaccinations or floating teeth, easy stuff like that, but if he has an emergency where he needs an extra set of hands, then I meet him there. So far, it's working out really well. I am so grateful he gave me this opportunity." Macy said, smiling over at Molly.

Molly then caught the girls up on the status of her next book which she was currently working on. *Lexington: A Novel*, had debuted earlier in the year and had been a smash hit. A screenwriter had recently gotten in touch with Molly, and they were in talks about turning the book into a movie. Molly was overjoyed.

"Are you almost finished with your current draft?" Asked Karen. "You know I can't wait to read it."

"I'm about halfway there," Molly answered. "I'm nervous though; I really like this one so far, but I don't think I'm going to be able to top *Lexington*. I just felt different when I was writing it, if that makes sense. Maybe it was because I was actually in Lexington, I'm not sure."

"I think it was because you were all lit up inside. You were falling in love with Beau," Macy said with a smile. "I think you had finally experienced real love for the first time. Of course you felt different."

Molly smiled back at her friend, remembering last summer when her whole life changed. "Yes, that is true. Beau is certainly my first *real* love."

The girls spent the next hour talking with Karen until Erin got up to leave. She had dinner plans with Kevin and some other friends in the city. Macy had whispered to her before she left. "Call me if you ever need to talk." Erin promised that she would.

As Macy made her way to her own car, Karen came out after her. "Macy, I almost forgot," she said, jogging across the front yard. "I ran into Mrs. Hutchinson at the feed store today, do you remember her? One of your mom's friends from the hunt club?"

"Oh of course. I used to ride with her daughter, Elise."

"That's right, of course you remember her. Anyway, she mentioned that the club wanted to have a brief memorial for your mother during the Christmas Hunt Ball. She wants to invite you and Tommy but didn't want to upset you either. If you are uncomfortable with being there, then everyone would understand."

Macy thought for a moment. It had been years since she had attended a Hunt Ball, and now the first one she'd be home for, she'd be going without her mother. Life could be so unfair. But of course she'd want to celebrate her mom's life and legacy.

"I can't speak for Tommy, but I'll definitely be there. How thoughtful of them. I know my mom would have loved it," Macy said, her eyes misting up a little.

"Wonderful. I'm so happy to hear that you'll be there. It's not until December, but I wanted to give you a heads up." Karen said with a sad smile. "I'm so heartbroken that this happened to you and Tommy, but just know that Rick and I are so proud of you. You've handled everything with such grace," she said, reaching out and pulling Macy into a tight hug.

"Thank you," said Macy, tears rolling down her cheeks. "Thank you for everything you've done for me. I don't know where I'd be without you and your family."

~ Chapter 10 ~

The Indian Summer did not last long, and November tore in with freezing temperatures and light snow showers. Unless she was working, Macy had always returned home for Thanksgiving, but she was at a loss for what to do this year, the first year without her mom. She knew that she didn't want to host it herself. It would be too hard to prepare a big meal in the same kitchen and sit down at the same table without her mother's presence.

Thankfully, Karen saved the day and invited her, Tommy, and Cora to their farm. Tommy and Cora would be having dinner with Cora's parents at their home in downtown Annapolis, but they were going to try and swing by later for dessert.

Macy arrived early with Mint Julep in tow. "I hope you don't mind me bringing her. I felt bad leaving her home on a holiday."

Karen laughed. "Of course not, dear! She and Rugby can play while we finish cooking." Rugby was the Sorrensons' black lab. He was only a year old, so the two pups tore off through the house, wreaking joyous havoc.

Macy had brought a pumpkin pie and an apple pie, both homemade, cool whip, and a bottle of Riesling. Beau helped her carry the treats in from her car and the two briefly discussed one of their patients.

"Monica called me earlier. Trooper finally passed some manure and seems to be improving," Beau told her. Trooper was a twenty-five year old Quarter Horse who had colicked earlier the previous day. Both Beau and Macy had spent most of the day with him.

"Oh thank goodness," Macy said, relief evident on her face. "I was praying he'd improve. No one wants to lose a pet on a holiday." Throughout the year, she'd had to put plenty of horses to sleep on holidays. Illness doesn't know what day it is, and nor does it care.

"Everything smells delicious," said Rick approvingly as he walked into the kitchen. He barely had the lid off a pot before Karen swatted at him.

"Oh no you don't!" She cried. "No free samples here. All men, out of the kitchen at once!" She said, shooing Beau and Rick away.

Macy and Molly laughed at Karen who was fiercely guarding her meal.

Erin and Kevin arrived shortly thereafter, and the women went about setting an absolutely beautiful table in the formal dining room. The room was large with dark brown hardwood floors. There was a stately stone wood-burning fireplace which Beau had stacked high with logs and was getting ready to light. Festive pumpkins, gourds, and decorative Indian cornhusks abounded.

Karen had outdone herself. With two turkeys and every side dish imaginable, their Thanksgiving dinner could only be described as a true feast. The family sat together and held hands while Rick offered the blessing. Macy teared up for a moment while Rick was praying; she couldn't believe that her mother wasn't here. That she wasn't back at her house at this minute, slaving away over her own meal, drinking hot apple cider, and laughing with her mom.

Molly squeezed Macy's hand and gave her an understanding smile. She knew what her friend was thinking.

Soon everyone was passing plates and serving others and Macy laughed at the large mound of food heaped on her plate. The Sorrensons certainly knew how to cook! Before she could dive in, Erin raised her glass to offer a toast to her mom who had worked so hard to create such a perfect dinner.

"Hear, hear!" Macy chimed as they clinked glasses.

"So, Mace," Erin said as she added some gravy to her mashed potatoes. "Did you know that your neighbor is a big-shot racehorse trainer?"

"I knew that he was a trainer, but that's it. What's he done?"

"He won the Derby six years ago on Happygolucky, remember that horse? Molly was in love with him because he was a striking dappled grey."

Molly perked up at the mention of this. "Oh, my goodness, that's right! Adam Cleary was his trainer. I can't believe I didn't put two and two together. I was obsessed with that horse!" She laughed to herself.

"Wow," Macy said with a slight smirk. "I didn't realize I was living next door to a celebrity. That explains why he's an arrogant, pompous pain in the butt."

When Macy saw Karen's confused look, she realized that only Molly knew of her run-ins with Adam. She quickly explained to the family about him wanting to buy her farm.

"He approached you only three weeks after Hadley died?" Karen asked. "That was pretty poor taste."

"Honestly, I think he's basically a nice guy, but there is just something about him. We do *not* mix. He always seems to say something that makes me want to hit him over the head with a shovel."

Erin laughed. "That sounds like marriage to me!" She said, giving Kevin a sly grin. He smiled back at her. Macy hoped that meant things between them were improving.

Tommy and Cora arrived just as Macy and Molly were bringing out the desserts. When asked if she cared for any wine, Cora responded, "I wish, but I can't drink at the moment." She grinned happily at the Sorrensons while she waited for them to put it together. She was almost three months along, so she felt comfortable telling family and close friends.

"Cora!" Karen shouted from across the room, her faced wreathed in a huge smile. "What are you saying?" She made her way around the table with her arms out, ready to hug the mom-to-be.

Cora laughed and pulled her shirt tight to show her tiny bump protruding. "I'm almost three months!" She was positively glowing.

"Congratulations!" Sang Karen who brought both Tommy and Cora into a big hug. Everyone gathered around to congratulate the happy couple. In the midst of all the hugging, handshaking, and back-slapping, Macy glanced over at Erin. Erin winked at her and mouthed, "it's okay."

Then Karen got down to business serving the desserts. "Cora gets an extra-large piece of pie since she's eating for two!"

As Macy looked around at her loving friends who had become family, she felt grateful. It had been a horrendous year, and she and Tommy had suffered an unimaginable loss, but she was so thankful that they had people like the Sorrensons in their lives. And in just a few more months, she was going to become an Aunt, which was definitely something she was looking forward to.

~ Chapter 11 ~

Macy looked at the clock; it was six-thirty in the evening. Molly and Beau would be picking her up for the Hunt Ball in fifteen minutes, but she was basically ready. The Ball was held just down the street at the Hunt Club, and even though Macy was saddened to be attending without her mother, she was excited to get out of the house and mingle with old friends.

The affair was black-tie, so a trip to the mall had been in order since Macy didn't have anything appropriate for the fancy party. She and Molly had gone together and made a day out of it, and Macy was pleased with her purchase. Now she stood in front of the full-length mirror in her room, her childhood room – she hadn't been able to bring herself to move into her mother's old room – and twirled around.

She admired the reflection. Macy had chosen an ice blue, full-length gown with a high neck. The dress fit her snuggly until just below the hips where it flared out, making it so she could move her legs freely if she ended up dancing a bit. While the collar fit her neck tightly, she didn't feel like she was being choked. The gown was also sleeveless and, mostly, backless. She was showing more skin than usual, but the dress had matched her eyes so perfectly that she couldn't pass it up.

Macy's naturally curly blonde hair made things easy in the updo department. She piled it high on her head and held it in place with multiple bobby pins. A few ringlets escaped on either side of her ears and at the nape of her neck.

Make up was also pretty simple as Macy hardly ever wore any, and tonight would be no real exception. Some eye shadow, liner, and mascara was about all she needed. Her lip gloss had a red hue to it, so she'd just use that. A spritz of her favorite perfume and mom's diamond stud earrings, and she was ready to go. Macy wanted to look her best on the night her mom was to be honored at the club that had meant so much to her.

"Wow, you look amazing!" Molly said when she knocked on the door a few minutes later.

"Thanks! You look pretty wonderful yourself!" Molly was a vision in an emerald green, form-fitting gown. "I bet Beau can't keep his eyes off you!"

Molly laughed. "His eyes *and* his hands," she said with a wink.

The party was already swinging when they walked through the doors of the club. Festive Christmas décor decorated every room, banister, and doorway. Macy especially loved the trees, one in each main room, that were bulging with lights and ornaments. It was hard not to feel the holiday cheer at every corner.

The three soon found their table where they met up with Tommy, Cora, and Molly's parents.

"Erin should be here in a few," said Karen. "Kevin had a work emergency, so he won't be able to make it."

"Good," said Macy. "Erin can be my date."

Erin arrived shortly before dinner was served, and the group talked happily about everyone's favorite subject, horses. As Macy looked around the club, filled to the brim with blissful members, she thought that maybe next year she'd start hunting again. It had been ages since she'd been out foxhunting.

Molly looked over at Macy with a twinkle in her eye. "Are you thinking what I'm thinking?" She asked with a smile.

Macy smiled back. "If you're thinking that it would be a great idea to start foxhunting regularly, then yes, I'm thinking what you're thinking!"

"Yes! How fun would that be? I wonder if Gypsy would be ready for the latter half of this season, second flight, of course. And maybe you could take Fitz next season once he's healed."

"That's exactly where my thoughts were going. I definitely think Hunter has it in him to hunt a season or two, but Fitz is so much younger. If he has the mind for it, I think he could be my guy."

"And I think it's about time I got out of the city more and breathed this wonderful country air," Erin chimed in. "I'm in too. Just need to find a horse first." Erin had looked a little frazzled when she had arrived, and Macy wondered if she and Kevin had been arguing. As soon as she got a chance to pull Erin aside to talk in private, Macy intended to ask her how things were going.

The three girls excitedly chatted about their foxhunting future when Arthur Murdock, the Master of Foxhounds, took the microphone on their small stage. It was time for the club to honor Hadley.

Arthur began by recounting Hadley's many contributions to the club over the years, and he was then followed by three other members who shared some wonderful memories. At the end, Macy and Tommy were asked to join them onstage where they presented the two with a bouquet of flowers and a framed picture the hunt's official photographer had taken of Hadley at last year's Blessing of the Hounds. She was holding a tray of stirrup cups and had a handful of hounds gathered around her feet. She was smiling directly at the camera and could not have looked happier if she tried.

Macy's eyes grew misty as she accepted the picture, and together she and Tommy stared longingly at their beautiful, lost mother. Then Tommy stepped up the microphone.

He cleared his throat. "Macy and I want to thank all of you for the kindness, loyalty, and friendship this club has shown my mother over the years. Nothing gave her more pleasure than riding out with all of you, when she was able, and managing and participating in all of your social functions. From the bottom of our hearts, thank you so much for not only being dear friends, but for being members of our extended family."

Macy stepped up the microphone. "As my brother said, my mom truly loved each and every one of you like family. You have all been so gracious to us since she passed, and I can't tell you how much that has meant. I so wish," Macy said, her voice cracking. Tommy put his arm around Macy's shoulders, and she took a deep breath, regaining her composure. "I so wish that she could have been here joining us tonight, but I know that she's here in spirit. Tommy and I would like to thank you all for honoring her, and thank you especially for this beautiful picture. It captures the true essence of her personality, and the love and affection she had for this club, perfectly."

Tommy leaned toward the microphone again. "Thank you all again, so much, and may you have a blessed Christmas holiday."

With that, the entire room stood up to cheer and didn't stop clapping until Tommy and Macy had returned to their seats. It had been beautiful tribute to a beautiful soul.

Arthur Murdock returned to the microphone and continued with the traditional ceremony, presenting a variety of awards and recognizing individuals for their support and assistance throughout the year thus far. When he was finished, he reminded all to participate in the silent auction. As he stepped off the stage, the lights were lowered, and the dancing commenced.

After chatting with a few members, Macy made her way to the silent auction tables. Immediately she spotted a print of a famous Franklin Voss painting and made a bid.

"I had my eye on that one too," said a voice behind her. "I hope you're prepared to fight for it."

Macy turned around to see her neighbor, Adam Cleary, standing before her looking incredibly dapper in a black tuxedo.

"You know I'm always ready for a good fight," said Macy with a smirk.

Adam laughed. "Truer words were never spoken," he said with a twinkle in his eye. Macy moved aside and made an "after you" gesture. Adam stepped up to the table and wrote his bid. When he finished he turned to her. "If I may say so, you look beautiful this evening," Adam said, genuinely.

Macy was caught off guard for a moment. She hadn't expected him to say anything pleasant, but rather throw another dig about the silent auction picture. Before she had a chance to respond, he asked her to dance.

"Oh no, I don't think that would be a good idea," she said, finally finding her voice.

"Why not?" He said, taking her hand and leading her to the dance floor anyway. "Neighbors are allowed to be nice to one another, you know. What do you say we start over, again? Third time's the charm and all that."

Before Macy had a chance to respond, Adam had pulled her close to him, almost too close for her comfort, and was moving in time to the slow dance song being played. She marveled at how smoothly he moved, and, surprisingly, at how natural it felt to be in his arms. The two molded together perfectly, blending into one.

When she looked up into his eyes, she found him staring straight into hers, his normally light blue eyes dark and mysterious. Macy couldn't believe it but found that she was at a loss for words.

Finally, she broke eye contact and said, "I agree. Neighbors should be nice to each other. I'm game for starting over, again, but," she looked back at him slyly, "this is your last shot."

Adam lowered his head until he was speaking directly into her ear and whispered, "I won't screw this up, I promise." After he spoke, he didn't lift his head, but kept his face close to hers, and they danced like that, almost cheek-to-cheek, until the song was over.

Macy realized that she was reluctant to pull away and noticed that Adam seemed disappointed that their time together was drawing to a close.

"Thank you for the dance," Macy said, a little shyly. "It was…unexpectedly nice."

"Indeed it was," Adam said with a mock bow.

As Macy walked out of the room, she was joined immediately by Molly, who looked like she was bursting with a million questions.

"Did I just see you dancing, and awfully closely, I might add, with your arch-enemy?" Molly asked, eyes shining with curiosity.

Macy blushed the tiniest shade of red. "Yes, you did," she said. "He asked and pulled me out onto the floor before I could think of a good reason not to."

Molly put her arm around her best friend. "You don't have to explain to me. It's okay if your hate relationship has moved up a notch into the love-hate category," she said, laughing to herself.

"You are terrible!" Macy said, pretending she was angry. "I still hate him, don't you worry."

Molly winked. "It's okay if you don't."

The rest of the evening was lovely. Macy danced with her brother and Mr. Sorrenson, and then she snuck away to talk with Erin for a few minutes. Sadly, Erin told her that she and Kevin were having more bad days than good again. They were, however, going to therapy together, but she wasn't sure it was helping much. When one spouse wants a child and the other does not, there really isn't much room for compromise.

"And it's not like I can say that I've never wanted kids. Before we got married, I told him that I'd most likely want them one day. So he went into this marriage thinking one thing, and now I'm throwing the complete opposite at him." Erin looked at her wit's end and was struggling not to cry.

The two girls talked for a while and both agreed that they'd still keep things under wraps until after the holidays. Erin was keeping Molly abreast of the situation, but she didn't want to worry her parents. If they were still fighting constantly after the New Year, then she'd fill them in.

Once they walked back into the main room, they realized that the silent auction had ended.

"Oh rats!" Sighed Erin. "I had meant to check on one of my items before it ended. Damn."

All of the bid sheets had been taken up, so there was no way of knowing the winners until they were announced. Macy knew for a fact that she hadn't won the picture though. She had meant to double back after her dance with Adam to place a higher bid, but she had forgotten.

Not surprisingly, Adam won the picture. As he carried it back to his table, he looked over the crowd at Macy and nodded with a smile. Macy, showing she was a good sport, raised her glass to him and nodded back.

Later as they pulled up to Macy's house and she got out of Beau and Molly's car, Macy realized that she had had a fantastic night. The tribute to her mother had been heart-wrenching, but it had also brought some closure. Seeing old friends celebrate her mother had been just what the doctor ordered.

Macy waved the two off and unlocked her front door. She had just taken two steps inside when she heard another car enter her driveway. Thinking that Beau or Molly had forgotten to tell her something, Macy turned around with a smile. It faded quickly when she saw who it was, Adam.

Confused, Macy walked down the steps of her front porch to meet him.

"You left without saying goodbye," said Adam, pretending his feelings were hurt.

Macy smiled softly. "Not that you would believe it, but I actually looked around for you as I was walking out the door. I figured you had beat me out."

"I went back to your table, hoping you catch you, but you were already gone. I wanted to give you something." With that, he opened the door to his backseat and pulled out the Voss print he had won. "I'd love for you to have it."

Macy, incredibly touched, and shocked, put her hand to her chest. "Oh Adam, that's awfully sweet of you, but I can't accept it. You won it fair and square."

"Please," he said, pushing it in her direction. "I want you to have it. Please take it. Consider it a peace offering."

With that, Macy took the picture and smiled up at Adam, her neighbor, a man she had clearly misjudged.

"Thank you, so very much," she said, a little overcome with emotion. Tonight had been one for the books. "Would you like to come in? I believe I have some bourbon, and I definitely have tea."

"I'd love to."

~ Chapter 12 ~

They both decided to have some hot tea, and while Macy prepared two cups, Adam began arranging logs in the kitchen fireplace. The house had felt drafty when they walked in, and Adam declared he'd have them warmed up in no time.

"This is a wonderful house," Adam said, stepping back from the fireplace to admire his handiwork. The flames had burst to life, instantly heating up the cold kitchen. "Have you always lived here?"

Macy came over to warm herself by the fire. "Yes, I've only ever known this home. Well, minus my place in Kentucky. But this has always been *home*."

"Did you always know you'd leave Kentucky one day and come back to Maryland?" Adam asked, his gaze falling over Macy, standing beside him.

She nodded. "I did. I love Kentucky – it will always have a piece of my heart. But I knew I was ready to come home. Even before my mom died, I knew I'd be home within a year. It's a shame I didn't come home sooner," she sighed.

Adam tucked a stray curl that had fallen from her updo behind her ear. "We can't see into the future. Don't beat yourself up about it." He gently held her chin in his hand and tilted her face so he could look her directly in the eye.

At that moment, the kettle on the stove began to whistle, so Macy stepped away and busied herself with pouring the water into the teacups. After adding some honey to hers and one cube of sugar to his, she and Adam sat at the breakfast nook opposite the fireplace.

"This is very good, thank you," Adam said after taking a sip. He smiled over at Macy and gave a small laugh. “Just a few months ago, who would have thought that you and I would be sharing tea and talking nicely together?”

Macy laughed as well. “Right? Look at us now – so friendly, so refined.” She smirked. “I’ve only ever been able to envision myself strangling you!”

The two sat together for a long time, talking about their histories. Adam told her that he was originally from Saratoga Springs, New York, and that his father had been in the racing business. Adam always knew that he wanted to be a horse trainer. Ten years ago, when he was thirty-two, he moved just south of Middleburg, Virginia, and set up his racing operation, Cleary Stables.

“So what brought you to Maryland?” Macy asked, curious as to why he’d leave the beautiful Middleburg area.

“Convenience. I was spending all of my time at Pimlico, Laurel, or Delaware Park. It just made sense for me to move north and set up shop somewhere in the middle. And now I’m even closer to Monmouth, Aqueduct, and Belmont.”

“You’ve been here, what, about six months now? Do you like it?”

“Yep, seven months next week,” Adam said with a smile. And looking directly into her eyes, he said, “I love it. The people up here can be hard to get to know, but they’ve grown on me.”

Macy grinned. “I’m not too sure what to tell you about that. We’re normally a pretty friendly bunch.”

And with that, Adam leaned closer to Macy, reached out his hand, and cupped her chin. He stared at her straight in the eye, and, tantalizingly slow, brought his lips down to meet hers. Macy was stunned for a moment but gathered herself quickly and began kissing Adam back. At first, hesitantly, then fiercely.

A slight moan escaped Macy's lips, and Adam slowly pulled away. "Sorry about that," he said huskily, his face still close to hers. "I don't know what came over me."

Macy could not believe that she had let herself kiss this man. This man that she had disliked so intensely. She thought them total opposites. But even still, none of that stopped her from sliding closer to him and kissing him again, this time as the aggressor, running her fingers through his hair and pulling him near.

Before she knew it, she was sitting on top, straddling him, and kissing him with more passion than she had intended. After a few minutes, he pulled away.

"The last thing I want to do is break this up, but I really think I should. I don't want us to get carried away." He looked as if saying that took every last bit of effort he had left. His hands lingered on her behind.

"What's so wrong with getting carried away?" Macy asked, still shocked at her behavior. In the back of her mind, she registered the fact that this was extremely unlike her. She had never initiated sex with a practical stranger. But tonight, she didn't care. "I'm game if you are…neighbor."

With that, Adam's eyes turned a deeper shade of blue, dark and lustful. The two extracted themselves from their seats somehow without extracting themselves from each other. With one smooth motion, Adam scooped Macy up in his arms and asked her where they should go.

"Upstairs to the right," was all she said.

By the time they made it to her bedroom, Macy had already let down her hair. Her mass of curls fell down her back, and Adam paused for a moment to really look at Macy as he laid her on the bed.

"You are so beautiful," he whispered. When her evening gown and his tuxedo had fallen to the floor, the two were already in bed, Adam on top of her, Macy moaning loudly. Within a matter of seconds, he was inside her, and Macy was moving her hips under his.

Ending up in bed together was the last thing Macy thought would happen tonight, but, as she had told Molly recently, Macy was having trouble recognizing herself. She felt different. And while being underneath Adam Cleary so soon wasn't something she'd normally do, she didn't care. Tonight, this felt right. How she'd feel tomorrow, well, that was another story.

As Adam kissed her neck, Macy arched her back up under him, rising up to meet each of his thrusts. She wrapped her legs around his waist, pushing him as deeply inside her as possible. She surprised herself with how much she wanted this man.

After a few minutes, they changed positions with Adam on lying on his back and Macy sitting on top. She rode him hard, bouncing up and down, holding his hands in hers, fingers intertwined. Adam leaned forward and took her breast in his mouth and sucked until she climaxed.

When Adam finished shortly thereafter, they lay next to each other, both out of breath and spent. Adam looked over at her, smiled broadly and softly caressed her cheek.

Macy looked back at him and sighed. *What have I done?*

~ Chapter 13 ~

"You did what!" Shouted Molly over the phone when Macy called her the following afternoon. "You had sex with your nemesis neighbor? But Mace, you hate him!"

"I know," Macy said, her voice cracking, tears ready to spill over. "I told you, it's like I don't know what I'm doing anymore. I have no control over myself."

Before she could continue, Molly interrupted. "Wait, I'm coming over. Be there in two."

After she hung up with Molly, Macy walked outside to the barn, Julep trotting briskly at her heels. It was two o'clock in the afternoon, too early for the horses' evening feeding, but she wanted to be where she felt most comfortable as she talked with Molly about how her life was falling into shambles. It was a relatively warm day for early December with the temperatures floating into the mid-fifties, but Macy still bundled up in her favorite sweatshirt and vest, an all-black, fleece-lined Ariat. She was still wearing her lined breeches from her ride on Hunter earlier that morning.

The horses nickered to her as she walked through the entrance of the old fieldstone barn. Not surprisingly, Macy loved this barn more than the house as she had probably spent more hours outside in it as she was growing up. Walking inside, she was greeted by the familiar smells of leather, pine shavings, hay, and the sweet tang of manure. The barn boasted a wide, expansive center aisle with six stalls on either side. To the right as she walked in was the large, wood-paneled tack and feed room. To the left was the wash stall, complete with hot and cold water. The loft was open and airy and was big enough to house hundreds of bales of hay.

Macy had enjoyed her light hack on Hunter through the trails earlier that morning; she had needed it after last night. She still couldn't believe she had slept with Adam. *I'm losing it*, she thought sadly as she pulled Fitz from his stall and placed him in cross-ties in the aisle. The gelding was healing well but still had about two more months of stall rest to go. Most horses would have been livewires after having been cooped up in their stalls for four months, but Macy had to hand it to Fitz. He had handled everything in stride. The move to Maryland. Being in his stall almost twenty-hour/seven. A brand new life, but he was just as sweet and loving as ever.

She unbuckled Fitz's light sheet and admired his striking dappled grey coat. At five, his coat was still dark and beautiful. Unfortunately, as grey horses age, their coats lighten up from the sun, and most end up turning completely white. Still, Macy loved grey horses, especially when their manes and tails were as black and thick as Fitz's.

Rooting through her caddy, Macy picked a dandy brush and got to work on Fitz's coat. Unlike some thin-skinned thoroughbreds, Fitz loved to be brushed and leaned into her caresses. When she scratched his favorite spot, high on his withers, he lifted his nose, lips twitching in pleasure.

"He's just darling," Molly's voice came from the top of the barn. "I'm so glad you saved him."

Macy smiled as she walked over to Molly and hugged her friend. "Me too. He didn't deserve to be put down just because his owner ran out of money. Poor guy. I hate to think about all the other thoroughbreds in Fitz's position out there who aren't as lucky." Macy sighed as she went back to work grooming her horse. Molly picked up a comb and started in on Fitz's tail. The horse, pleased with so much attention, eyed both girls happily.

"You like your spa day, huh, handsome boy?" Macy asked, giving him a pat on his neck.

The girls worked in silence for a few minutes with Molly taking a moment to say hello to Hunter, who was contentedly munching on hay in his stall. Then she spoke.

"So, Mace, what's going on?" Her voice was soft and sad. She knew her friend was hurting, knew that her life had been turned upside down after her mother's passing.

Macy looked up from picking one of Fitz's hooves and looked like she was on the verge of tears. "Moll, it's like I said on the phone, sometimes I just don't recognize myself. I can't control what I do, what I say. I think one thing, and then I do the exact opposite."

"It's okay, Mace. You've got to understand that you're still grieving. You've suffered the biggest loss of your life. It would be strange if you were completely fine now, only four months later. You need to cut yourself some slack."

"I know. And you're right. But last night…? What the hell was I thinking?"

"What happened exactly? He wasn't pushy, was he?" Molly asked seriously.

Macy gave a small laugh. "Oh goodness no. Quite the opposite, as a matter of fact. I didn't give him much of a chance to say no." She told Molly how Adam had arrived shortly after she returned home to give her the picture. Macy had been so touched by his thoughtfulness that she invited him in for a drink.

"And we had tea, for goodness sake! It's not like I can even blame it on alcohol. I only had one glass of wine earlier in the evening." When Molly started to laugh, Macy joined in. "Who knew tea could be such an aphrodisiac!" She laughed, shaking her head. "But seriously, he did nothing wrong. He leaned in to kiss me first, but I took it from there. There was even one moment when he said he'd better leave before things got out of hand, but I told him to stay. What was I thinking?"

"Maybe you don't hate him as much as you thought," Molly said with a smile. "And you know what else? You're both adults – you can do whatever you want, and you shouldn't feel bad about it. If you want to see him again, go for it. If not, then don't." Molly came around and put her hands on Macy's shoulders, looking the girl straight in the eye. "You don't have to have all the answers today. You are allowed to take as much time as you'd like to figure everything out. Your whole life has changed in a matter of weeks. You lost your mom. You left the place you called home for almost a decade. You have added two members to your family," she grinned, looking at Fitz and Julep, who was chasing a mouse across the aisle. "Give yourself some *time*."

Macy nodded. "You're right. I haven't been in my right mind since your wedding. That was the last time my life felt normal, like *mine*, you know? Since then, I feel like I've been clinging to a life raft, desperately trying to keep from drowning. I just feel so out of control, so…lost. I flipped out at work, left my job in a hurry, came home with a second horse – for whom I'm grateful," she said quickly with a smile, scratching Fitz behind the ears. "And even though I was reckless last night, I also have to admit that I enjoyed myself too. I *am* very attracted to Adam…and it was nice to, I don't know, do something a little out of character for me. Well, I guess I've been doing quite a bit that's been out of character for me," she said with a smirk.

"You're allowed to enjoy yourself, Mace. Even though things have been so rough, you don't have to feel like you need to grieve forever. Hadley wouldn't have wanted that. She would want you to move forward, be happy, ride horses, rescue dogs – you know how she was!" Molly laughed as she went to work combing Fitz's mane. "It's going to take some time, but you will heal. And you have to let yourself heal too. Let yourself be happy. Let yourself do whatever you need to do to heal. If that means hanging out with your hunky neighbor, do it. As we say in the horse world, you have to keep kicking on!" she said with a wink.

"When did you get so smart?" Macy asked with a playful smile. "I mean, I always knew you were intelligent, but you always know just what to say. Thank you, Molly. I love you for always being here for me."

"Just returning the many favors," she said. "You were there for me two summers ago when I needed to get out of Maryland. You opened your door to me without hesitation."

Macy laughed. "I was just happy to have some good company!"

"So what do you think you'll do about the dashing Mr. Cleary?" Molly asked, a wicked smile playing across her lips.

Macy smiled back. "I really don't know. I think I'm going to leave the ball in his court. Part of me thinks I'm playing with fire, but the other part of me could really use the distraction."

Molly giggled as she stepped back to survey her handiwork. Fitz's mane sparkled. "Do what you need to do, my love. Just be *happy*."

~~~~~

Later that evening, Macy's cell phone rang as soon as she walked out of the shower. After Molly had left, Macy had spent the rest of the afternoon outside with
~~~~~

the horses, feeding around five, their normal dinner time, and taking Julep for a long walk around the perimeter of her property. When she walked along the side adjacent to Adam's farm, she hid behind a tree and did a little spying. She had laughed to herself remembering how she and Tommy loved to sneak around, spying on their neighbors. *What strange kids we were!*

From her vantage point, she could only see the back of white fenced pastures with the barn atop the hill, off to the right. No sign of life. She wasn't surprised that she hadn't heard from Adam and wasn't sure she even wanted to. Then Macy realized that neither had the other's cell numbers, and Macy no longer had a house phone.

Macy, towel wrapped around her wet hair, reached her phone just before it clicked over to voicemail. It was Cassidy.

"Hi!" Macy said excitedly. It had been a few weeks since she had spoken to her friend. "I'm so glad you called – I've missed you!"

Macy could hear Cass smile through the phone. "Me too – I've missed your voice! I'm sorry we haven't been able to catch up recently. Work has been crazy, and I believe we've been playing phone tag."

"I have some news for you," Macy said, thinking there was no reason she couldn't tell Cass about her strange romance with Adam. It would be good to have another perspective. "But first, tell me, how are you? How's the hospital? Any news?"

Cass filled Macy in on the current hospital drama, which wasn't that dramatic, but still, Macy missed her former colleagues and wanted to hear about their comings and goings. She was saddened to hear that one of her favorites, Whitney, had taken a job in California.

"Oh bummer. I wish I would have known. I

couldn't have made it to her going away party, but I would have sent a note," said Macy. "And what about you? Any thoughts about where you want to spend your residency?"

"I've applied to Hagyard, of course, but I've also applied to Cornell and New Bolton. My parents are irate about the fact that I might move to New York or Pennsylvania, but I've had enough. I love it here, of course, and Hagyard is right down the street, but New Bolton would be my preference. How far is that from you?"

"About an hour, so not too bad! Fingers crossed you get it. I've been there before, and it's amazing."

"How's the lovely Fitz?" Cassidy had supported Macy after she had told her what happened in Roy's office. She couldn't believe his owner was serious about putting him down and told Macy she had absolutely made the right decision.

"He's perfection. He's just a big, sweet teddy bear. It's like he knows that I saved him from a sad fate, you know? And his tendon looks great and his suspensory is still healing. He'll be good as new by spring."

"I'm so happy to hear it. And I truly believe horses are smarter than anyone gives them credit for – I bet he knows that you rescued him. I miss that love bug."

"Well that just means you need to come visit him!"

"Actually, I was going to suggest that! If I get an interview with New Bolton, I was hoping I could stay with you for a few days."

"You know you are always more than welcome."

"Now it's your turn. How are you? You sound like you have some interesting news."

Macy took a deep breath and told Cassidy all

about Adam. How, until she recently, she hadn't been a fan of his, how he had come across as arrogant and abrasive. But then how kind and caring he had been at the Hunt Ball. Macy admitted that, initially, she had been too quick to fight with him, how she had been looking for an excuse to take all her pain and anger and frustration out on someone. He just happened to be the one to knock on her door, literally.

"So this all happened last night? Like, less than twenty-four hours ago?"

"Yes, just last night. We danced at the Ball and, I don't know, things just felt different, and I was starting to regret my behavior towards him. I watched him with other friends and club members, and I could tell that he is genuinely well-liked. I mentioned him to one of my mom's old friends, and she simply raved about what a great guy Adam was. So, that got me thinking that it wasn't him so much as it was *me*."

"And then he showed up afterward with the picture?"

"He did indeed. And then we talked for a while, and he was so nice and easy to talk to. I don't know why that didn't come across the first time I met him. But, as you know, I wasn't in the best frame of mind then."

"So, what are you going to do now?"

"Oh Cass, that is the million dollar question…of my life."

~~~~~

Cassidy had basically mirrored Molly's advice, which was to do whatever made her happy. Macy deserved to feel like she was a little "off her rocker," as Cass put it, but she was sure everything would right itself in good time.
~~~~~

Macy let Julep out once more before bed, and as she stood on the back deck gazing out across her farm, she knew in her heart that one day she'd overcome the tricks her mind was playing on her. But for now, she'd put her sorrows aside, try not to think about them, and stay as busy as possible. Tomorrow she was going Christmas shopping with Molly and Erin; the day would be a nice distraction.

~ Chapter 14 ~

"Oh, Mace, look," said Molly, holding up a baby onesie with horses printed on it. "You should get this for Cora; I bet she'd love it for the baby."

"Aww so cute! I'll take it." Macy took the onesie and placed it in her basket.

The girls had spent most of the morning at Towson Town Center, the mall closest to them, but were now shopping in Hunt Valley, about fifteen minutes north of Towson, but ten minutes away from their homes in Monkton.

The three girls didn't have large families, so they had been able to start and finish most of their shopping in just one day. The stores were fairly crowded, but not as terrible as they expected. They figured that most people did their shopping online now, and while it had been a fun day to be out in the hustle and bustle, they could understand why some chose to do their shopping from the comfort of their own homes.

"How about we grab a late lunch at Manor Tavern?" Erin suggested as she finished paying for a gift for her boss at the law firm. Macy and Molly readily agreed as both were starving.

The Manor Tavern, a restaurant located on Old York Road just down the street from their farms, was a long-time family favorite. The Tavern was originally built as a stable in 1750 and has experienced many transformations from a dirt-floor saloon to the full-service restaurant it is today. It is a local gem hidden in horse country.

Since it was two o'clock and the lunch rush had come and gone, the three girls had their pick of the tables and chose a large booth so they could spread out. Macy always enjoyed coming here not only because their food was fabulous, but she liked the general equestrian atmosphere. Paintings depicting horse races and steeplechases and framed jockey silks adorned the walls, and a large fire was roaring in the stone fireplace along the side wall.

All three ordered Irish coffees, looking forward to a hot drink with just a little kick. They also decided that some warm crab dip would be perfect to start, so they ordered a large serving to share.

"This has been such a nice day," Erin said, smiling at her sister and friend. "We should do this more often."

"Agreed," said Molly. "And you should get your butt back up here. I can't believe you've lived in the city for as long as you have."

"Trust me, I didn't want to stay after we got married, but Kevin just isn't ready to leave. He likes it out here, but he loves the convenience of the city."

"Any news with you two since we spoke at the Ball?" Macy asked.

"Not really," Erin said with a sigh. "We're at a complete stalemate. He's adamant that he wants kids, which he's always said. And I," she said sadly, "just don't. Which each passing day, I feel sure of the fact that I'm not meant to be a mother."

Molly reached across the table and took her sister's hand. "And you don't need to be one. All you need to do is what's right for you. And if not having kids is what's right for you, that's fine. Everything with Kevin will work out one way or the other."

"I think we're both coming to terms that it might not work out for us. We're thinking of separating. We want to stay in counseling and keep trying, but we're thinking of taking some time apart after the New Year."

"And you will stay with me," Macy said firmly. "Unless he's moving out and you want to stay in your apartment, you are more than welcome to move in with me for as long as you need. I could use the company."

Erin's eyes started to fill, but she refused to let her tears spill. She reached over and hugged Macy. "And I will take you up on that invitation…if it comes to that, of course."

With that, their drinks arrived and they placed their meal orders, all three deciding to just have an early dinner.

After the waitress left, Molly raised her glass. "I want to propose a toast to the two strongest and most wonderful women I know. This has been an incredibly tough year for both of you, but I know each of you will come out on the other side much stronger, wiser, and, most importantly, *happier* than you've ever been. And I will always be here for you two like you both have been here for me. I love you guys so much."

"I'll drink to that!" Erin said, grinning ear-to-ear.

"Cheers!" Said Macy as the three clinked their coffee mugs. "And we love you too."

Over their meals, Macy told Erin about her night with Adam. Erin, who, out of the three women, had always been the wild one who enjoyed a good party, encouraged Macy to continue seeing her neighbor. Her reasoning – *why not?*

"You two are both single, a little lonely, and old enough to understand what you're doing. If you want to get to know each other better, go for it. Who cares if you got off on the wrong foot initially? You now know that he's not as bad as you thought. Besides, it's almost winter. Why not spend the next few cold months snuggled up to a warm body?"

Erin always knew what to say to get a reaction out

of the others. At that comment, Molly's mouth dropped open, and Macy laughed hysterically.

"I wouldn't have put it like that exactly, but you do make an excellent point, Erin," said Macy, winking at her friend.

Three Irish coffees later, Macy was feeling a little silly and was happy that Molly was driving home. While they were waiting on the check, Macy went to the ladies' room, and upon passing the bar just to the right, she looked over and saw none other than Adam sitting at the bar. He looked up, but she quickly turned her head in the other direction, continuing on to the restroom.

Oh please don't let him have seen me! She thought as she finished up and washed her hands. Macy decided she'd head back to the table and wouldn't even glance over towards the bar. Hopefully he wouldn't see her, and she could escape unnoticed.

No such luck. She opened the door and there he was, leaning against the wall, arms folded, waiting for her.

He was wearing his Cheshire cat grin; his eyes were twinkling. "Now I know you weren't going to just slip out without saying hello, right?" His tone was mischievous, and her heart gave a little lurch.

She decided to lie. "What are you talking about? I didn't even know you were here," she said coolly.

"Come now, Ms. Holland. I saw you look over as you walked by."

"Why, Mr. Cleary, I'm afraid you are mistaken," she said with a sweet, innocent smile.

"Am I? Well how about I come over tonight and we can talk about this mishap a bit more?" He asked hopefully.

"Uh…" Macy stammered. She hadn't expected this. "Uh…I can't tonight. I'm sorry. I have other plans."

"Tomorrow night?"

"Can't. More plans."

"Well how about this. How about I get your cell number so I can give you a call, and you can continue to tell me about all these plans you have – sound good?"

Macy had to give him credit. He had trapped her. She couldn't very well refuse to give him her number. But when she remained silent, he continued.

"I need your number, Macy. What if one of your horses gets out of the fence and I need to alert you?"

"Okay fine, you win."

After he punched her number into his phone, he thanked her, leaned forward, kissed her on her cheek, and was gone.

~~~~~

Adam called later that evening, but Macy sent it to voicemail. "Hey Mace, it was nice running into you this afternoon. I know you said you had *plans* tonight and tomorrow, but I'd like to get together again. I can cook at my house if you'd like. Anyway, call me when you can."

Macy was so very tempted to call him back. She could think of nothing other than showing up at his house and asking him to give her a tour of his bedroom. But she couldn't.

She agreed with Erin that she was an adult and could do whatever she wanted, but one of her comments at lunch at had Macy worried. *You're both single, a little lonely, and old enough to understand what you're doing.* Macy did understand what she was doing, but recently, she didn't feel like she could *control* what she was doing. And until she could get a better grip on herself and her life in general, she'd have to stay on her side of the property line. Eventually Adam would get the hint.
~~~~~

~ Chapter 15 ~

"Hold her here for a sec, would you, Mace?" Beau asked as he handed her a lead rope. They were on a call at a nearby farm stitching up a horse who had badly cut herself on a fence nail. The horse was a beautiful dark bay mare with a striking white blaze marking the center of her refined face.

"I can't believe I didn't see that nail sticking out," said the Emily, horse's owner. "I swear I check these things regularly. And now look at her, my poor Gemma." Emily looked like she was ready to cry as she stroked the horse's neck and ruffled her mane.

Macy reached out and put a hand on Emily's arm. "It's okay. Don't beat yourself up – these things happen. Besides, Beau is the best, scarring will be minimal." The cut was along the mare's shoulder; it was about six inches long and relatively deep. Beau was in the process of disinfecting the wound site before he got to work repairing it.

Beau smiled at them. "Don't worry yourself, Emily. These kinds of things happen all the time," he said reassuringly. "It's a deep cut, but I've seen much worse. She'll live," he said with a wink.

Macy and Beau worked together until Gemma was stitched up and as good as new. They gave her some pain killers and antibiotics to ward off the chance of infection.

"Thank you two for coming so quickly. I was worried you'd be on vacation or something with Christmas in two days," said Emily.

"It's no problem at all," said Beau easily. "My practice consists of just the two of us, so one or the other will be on call throughout the holidays. We've got y'all covered."

"That makes me feel so much better," said Emily, looking relieved. "But fingers crossed I won't have to call you!"

Beau and Macy talked easily as they made their way to their trucks and packed up all their equipment. Unless any emergencies came through, they were done for the day. It was cold but sunny in Maryland, a typical late December day. The leaves had fallen from the trees weeks ago, and the air hung tight and crisp. The sun shining away, however, made it all bearable.

"So, what are your plans for the holidays," Beau asked as he finished updating Gemma's records. "Molly said you're joining us for Christmas Day, but I assume you'll be seeing Tommy at some point."

"Yes, Tommy and Cora are coming over to the house for breakfast on Christmas morning. We're going to try and get together on Christmas Eve for church too, but I guess that depends on what's going on here since I'm on call that night. Hopefully it will be quiet. And then, yes, I'll be over with you guys for Christmas dinner. I can't thank Karen enough for including me. I have to admit, this is going to be tougher than I thought. I get teary-eyed every time I think about it being my first Christmas without my mom," Macy said, her eyes starting to shine.

Beau looked at his friend thoughtfully and nodded. "I'm sure. I can't imagine how that feels but know that you're not alone. You have us, Mace. We'll always be here for you and Tommy."

Macy smiled at Beau. "I know. I am so thankful for all of you. You've truly become my family."

~~~~~
~~~~~

When Macy returned home not long after, the sun was still out and the wind was quiet. *I'm going to go for a quick ride before dark*, she thought happily. She had about an hour and a half until the sun set behind the trees to the west of her property.

Macy turned on the radio inside the barn and found the station that played Christmas music 24/7. She sang softly to one of her favorites, "Have Yourself a Merry Little Christmas," and tacked up Hunter. Fitz hung his head over the stall door, and Macy patted him lovingly every time she walked by. She loved her two boys more than anything.

"Just you wait," she told Fitz as she planted a quick kiss on his nose. "You'll be good as new in no time, and I'll be tacking you up for some fun rides out cross country. You're going to be my foxhunter, did I tell you that?" She laughed as Fitz looked back at her as if he was truly interested.

Since it was cold out and Hunter wasn't clipped, Macy took the ride nice and easy. If she rode hard and Hunter started to sweat, it would take forever for him to dry out with his shaggy winter coat. She didn't plan on riding hard this winter, so she had decided not to clip him. And besides, Hunter was nearing his mid-twenties, so it was time to start taking it a little easier on the old guy.

Trotting down the fence line towards the back end of her property, Macy took in the scenery about her. Even though the trees were bare and the grass was almost dead, winter still had a beauty about it. The air seemed clearer, cleaner, the lines of the trees and sky, crisper. Summer was definitely her favorite season, but she did think that she wouldn't appreciate summer quite as much without winter's opposition.

After a short canter through the small trail on a

neighboring farm, Macy decided to head in before dark. She gave Hunter his head and he stretched down low, walking for a few strides with his nose close to the ground. The walk back would be the perfect cool down since he wasn't that hot to begin with.

As she made her way out of the trail and into an open field, she noticed another horse and rider off in the distance. Judging by the rider's location, she figured it was Adam riding around on his property. Not wanting to be seen, she quickly turned back into the trail, deciding to make her way back around the trail and come out on the other side of her property.

Adam had sent her a few texts over the last week or two, but her replies had been very short. She had not wanted to encourage anything on either of their parts. He also had called her once, but she didn't answer, and he didn't leave a message.

Just as she was entering the head of the trail again, she heard the sound of hoof beats and then Adam called her name. *Crap, he saw me.*

He galloped at a fast clip towards her, and then trotted the rest of the way up to her so as not to spook Hunter. He was riding a leggy blood bay without a single white marking. The horse was gorgeous.

"You weren't trying to run back into the trail and hide from me, now were you?" He asked with a sly grin. He had clearly seen her the entire time.

"Why no," she lied. "I didn't even know you were out riding. I was just going to make another loop around the trail before dark." She smiled sweetly to try and throw him off.

"Mind if I join you?" He asked, squeezing his legs to signal the horse to move off at the walk. He wasn't going to give her a chance to turn him away.

The two settled into a relaxing walk, the horses

walking side-by-side through the wide trail. Macy noted with satisfaction that Adam was an excellent rider. His form was impeccable; he was a natural.

"So, who do we have here?" Macy asked, nodding at Adam's horse.

"This is Pitcher. He's my personal horse. One of my owners had him in training, and he just wasn't cutting it as a racehorse. I exercised him quite a bit and fell for him. When the owners decided to rehome him, I couldn't resist. I've had him about five years now, and he's just the best, very versatile. Foxhunter, track pony, you name it, he does it with ease."

"Just not racing," Macy laughed.

Adam laughed as well. "Right, just not racing. He does love a good gallop, as you just saw, but he's not competitive. I think he just got too nervous in the crush of all the other horses."

"That's possible. Some of the fastest horses just don't fire during a race for whatever reason. He's lucky that you adopted him. Although he's incredibly handsome and seems level-headed; he probably wouldn't have had a hard time finding another home. Not all retired racehorses are as lucky."

"I know, and it's really heartbreaking. I do everything I can to place mine out when their racing careers are over. I work with a bunch of OTTB adoption centers, and, at this point, I have a pretty large private network of foxhunters, eventers, steeplechase trainers, you name it, who are always looking for athletic Thoroughbreds."

Macy smiled. She liked that Adam seemed to be one of those trainers who did right by his horses. Not all trainers were as kind. "Good, I'm glad to hear it. I understand it's tough though – mixing horses and business isn't always pretty." She told him how she acquired Fitz.

"Wow, that's pretty insane. I can't believe he wasn't even willing to let you try and place him," he said, shaking his head in disbelief. "It's a good thing you were there to save him."

"Yes, it was. I mean, it's frustrating because I lost my job over it, but I couldn't let him die. I wasn't going to stand by and watch them put a perfectly good horse to sleep all because the owner was running out of money."

When Adam stayed quiet, Macy looked over to see him smiling back at her. Even with his riding helmet on and the setting sun, his blue eyes stood out, slicing right through her. He and his horse made a stunning picture. Macy felt her heart flutter a tiny bit and prayed that she could remove herself from this man before things got out of hand, again.

"Are you going home for Christmas?" Macy asked. She knew that Adam's parents still lived in Saratoga.

"I'm not," he said with a smirk. "My parents are actually on a cruise. This is the third year they've done this, so I'll just stay here and look after the horses. I gave most of my staff off. What are your plans?"

"Well I'm on call tomorrow night, so I'm not doing much. If I can get away, I'll meet my brother and sister-in-law at church. I'm spending Christmas Day with Molly's family."

"Why don't you come over for dinner tomorrow night? I don't know what it is, but I hate spending Christmas Eve alone. Being by myself on Christmas Day doesn't bother me one bit, but there's just something sad about spending Christmas Eve alone."

Macy hesitated. As much as she'd like to spend time with Adam, she knew it wasn't a good idea. "Thanks for the invitation, but, like I said, I'm on call. I'd hate to get there and have to run immediately."

"It's no problem. If you have to go, then go. But I'd love to have you over and show you what I've done with the place."

"Adam, I appreciate it, but…I don't think it's such a good idea."

"Why not? Please come. I'm actually a good cook. We'll eat dinner, and then you can head home whenever you'd like." He looked at her seriously. "No funny business, I promise. I'd just really like to have some company."

Macy sighed. She had to admit to herself that she didn't really want to be alone either. This holiday was going to be a rough one no matter what she did. "Okay, I'll join you for dinner. Let me know what I can bring."

"Just bring your pretty self – and your appetite."

~ Chapter 16 ~

Macy only had one call during the day on Christmas Eve, so she was home and in sweats by one o'clock in the afternoon. She put the tea kettle on, grabbed her favorite Christmas mug, and turned on the radio so cheerful, holiday tunes filled the air. She went outside to the wood pile, brought in a few logs, and started a fire in the kitchen fireplace. If her heart wasn't so heavy, she would have felt downright festive.

It was times like this that made Macy miss her mom the most. By this point, Hadley would have baked dozens of Christmas cookies, the three trees throughout the house would be lit, decorated to max capacity, and she'd have multiple dishes baking in the oven. The house would be a plethora of delicious smells between the food, the live greens and holly, and her favorite cinnamon-scented candles.

Macy hadn't put much effort into the holiday this year. She put electric candles in each of the front-facing windows, and put a spotlight on the front door, illuminating the large wreathe she had purchased at the local Christmas tree farm. As far as the inside, things looked pretty sparse. She just hadn't had it in her to decorate the trees, to pull out the ornaments and relive all those cherished, and now painful, memories over again. The stockings remained packed in the attic as well. She hoped that next year would be better.

With her steaming mug of peppermint tea ready to go, she rolled up her sleeves and started baking. She was making Derby Pie to take over to Adam's tonight, along with a bottle of Woodford Reserve's bourbon. Then she was going to make her mother's famous peanut butter fudge and sugar cookies to take to the Sorresons' tomorrow. Tommy was going to be the chef for breakfast the following day, so she didn't have to prep much for that.

Humming softly along with the song on the radio, she looked over to see her cell phone buzzing on the counter. It was a text from Adam.

Adam: Any special requests for tonight?
Macy: Nope, I'm not picky.
Adam: Crabcakes?
Macy: Perfect!
Adam: Figured a Maryland girl would enjoy that.
Macy: I'm bringing some pie. And alcohol.
Adam: Now we're talking!

Macy realized she was smiling to herself as she texted with Adam. She felt like a giddy schoolgirl, which scared her. She didn't know if she was ready to get involved with someone right now, especially a neighbor, someone she'd see on a somewhat regular basis.

After feeding the horses and taking Julep for a walk later that evening, Macy changed into a pair of dark blue skinny jeans, a plain, bright red long-sleeved sweater, and heels. She wore her curly hair down, noting how long it had gotten as it cascaded down her back. A simple pair of pearl earrings completed the look.

I'm putting way too much effort into this, she thought unhappily. *What are you doing, Mace?* She chastised herself. But then she remembered both Erin's and Molly's advice. She was an adult. She could do whatever she wanted, with whomever she pleased. Macy just hoped she wasn't making a huge mistake.

Adam had told her she could bring Julep, so she clicked the dog's leash onto her collar and loaded her, the pie, and the bourbon in the car. If she got an emergency call, she'd just dash back over and change into her barn clothes. *Fingers crossed it's a quiet night.*

She drove over to Adam's house, feeling silly for driving to a neighbor's. The temperature had dipped into the low thirties, and she was wearing heels, so those would be her excuses if Adam tried to make fun of her.

Adam's house, a classic Cape Cod, was a little smaller than hers, but what it lacked in size, it made up for in character. The house was built around the same time Macy's had been, close to a hundred years ago. The brick had been painted white, the shutters were black, and the large front door boasted a rich, deep red. Macy knew that the flower gardens, not in bloom now, that flanked the front porch were stunning the in spring and summer.

Macy knocked on the door with Julep sitting on the porch next to her like a little lady. Adam opened the door and smiled broadly. "Look at these two beautiful ladies," he said as he reached down to scratch Julep behind her ears. "I see you drove. How was traffic?" He asked sarcastically with a wicked smile.

"I knew you'd have something to say about that!" Macy said, swatting at Adam as she walked inside. "It's freezing outside. And I'm wearing heels, which isn't something I do often, so you should feel special."

Adam smiled sweetly down at her. "I do. I'm very happy you're here."

Macy blushed the tiniest shade of red as Adam helped her out of her coat and hung it in the closet. Unlike hers, Adam's house was decorated for the Christmas season. There was a large fire roaring in the living room fireplace, which was off to her right, and a large tree, decorated and lit with white lights, sat proudly in the opposite corner of the fire. A few holiday knick-knacks adorned the end tables and mantle. Macy was surprised that a single man would go to the trouble of decorating a house only he would see.

"It's so Christmas-y in here," Macy said, surveying the room with satisfaction. "I have to say, I didn't peg you as someone who decorated for the holidays."

"You got me," Adam said, looking sheepish. "I only decorated this morning because I knew you were coming. Most of this stuff belonged to my ex-wife, so I dug through some boxes in the attic until I found a few things."

"Oh, I didn't know you had been married."

"Yes, quite some time ago. We got married too young, right out of college, and just grew apart. She wasn't into horses or racing, so that didn't help either – not much in common. It was relatively amicable, if such a thing exists in a divorce."

"What was her name?" Macy was curious.

"Ava. We were college sweethearts at Cornell, got married the year we graduated. We were just babies. When I got ready to make the move to Virginia, she said she wouldn't be joining me." He shrugged then shook his head as he grinned. "I can't believe I kept all this Christmas stuff. I guess I'm a little more sentimental than I thought."

"Well I'm glad you did. Your place looks beautiful – thanks for decorating for me, although you didn't have to."

"I know, but I wanted to."

At that moment, a timer in the kitchen began to sound.

"Dinner's ready," Adam said as he made his way to the kitchen. Macy followed, bourbon and Derby Pie in hand. He had already set the dining room table, and while he brought the food to the table, Macy poured them each a glass of water and a glass of white wine.

"I figure we can have the bourbon with dessert, if that works for you."

"It absolutely does. Thanks for bringing it," Adam said. "Why don't you have a seat at the table? I just need to grab the potatoes, and we're good."

Macy admired the formal dining room. It was small, but large enough to contain a table and six chairs, a corner hutch loaded with dinnerware, and a small dry sink. On the table, Adam had placed a formal cloth and three tall candles in a silver candelabra. Christmas music drifted softly in from the TV in the living room.

Adam walked in with the potatoes au gratin casserole, steaming straight from the oven.

"As Molly would say, you get an A for presentation. The room is beautiful, and the food smells amazing. Thank you again for having me."

Adam smiled genuinely. "You are more than welcome. And like I said, you are doing me a favor. I don't like to be alone on Christmas Eve. I've been looking forward to this all day."

The meal was perfection. Adam had prepared Maryland-style crabcakes and filet mignons – steak and cake – as it was called. The potato casserole was paired with steamed broccoli, zucchini, and squash. A French baguette and béarnaise sauce for the steak completed the meal.

"This looks absolutely amazing. Did you really make all this yourself?"

"I sure did," Adam said. "I never have time for it, but I really enjoy cooking."

"Well, you've certainly impressed me." She took a bite of her crabcake. "Mm – divine," she said with her mouth full. "Well done, sir. Any Marylander would approve."

"Yeah, you Marylanders sure do seafood right.

Old Bay on everything."

"Yes! You don't know how badly I missed crabcakes and steamed crabs when I lived in Kentucky. No one does it like we do here at home."

The two had a lovely dinner with easy conversation. One topic just seemed to flow into the next, and Macy was reminded of that night at her house after the Hunt Ball. Adam, despite his occasional abrasiveness, actually made Macy feel very comfortable, very much at home. As her mom would have said, "He's a pleasant sort."

Adam talked a bit more about his ex and how he had wished her well. By the time they had separated, they both had known for a while that things weren't working out.

"Did you try to fix it? Did you go to counseling?" Macy asked, thinking in the back of her mind about Erin. She wondered what the latest was with her and Kevin.

"We did, but very briefly. We went to a counselor maybe a handful of times. It was pretty cut and dry by that point since we just wanted two separate things. I wanted to move and follow the racing circuit a bit more, and Ava wanted to settle down and have kids. I would have liked to have kids at some point too, but, at that time, my job came first."

"That's so sad. Not about your wanting a career, just that you couldn't work it out."

"It was, and in retrospect, I should have tried to compromise with her a bit more. But at that point, I think we were both just ready to move on. She remarried a few years later and has two small children. We don't really talk, but she lives pretty close to my parents in Saratoga. They ran into her not long ago and said she's doing very well – and I'm happy for her." Macy could tell that he really meant it.

After dinner, Macy cut slices of her Derby Pie, a specialty of hers she'd perfected while living in Kentucky, while Adam poured the bourbon. Macy requested just a tiny bit as she was still on call that night. She'd only had one small glass of wine with dinner as well.

"This pie is delicious," Adam said after a huge bite. "This is the first time I've had it."

"Really? You never tried it when you were in Kentucky for the Derby?" She couldn't believe it.

"Nope. I'm always so on edge that I can hardly eat while I'm there."

"I can definitely understand that."

Adam then told her about one of his horses in training, his Derby-hopeful. "His name is Etch A Sketch, and he's owned by a racing partnership not far from here. He came out swinging this year as a two year old and is undefeated. Unfortunately, he had an injury that kept him out of the Breeder's Cup Juvenile, but he qualified for it, which was impressive. He's back to normal now, but we're taking things very slow. If all goes well though, he'll run in a few derby prep races this spring."

Macy was thrilled to hear he had a derby prospect. After she had realized he was a pretty well-known trainer, Macy had done a little research on Adam's career. Of course he'd had his ups and downs, but overall he has had an exciting career as a trainer.

"Will I get to meet Etch A Sketch at some point? I have a thing for celebrities – horse celebrities, that is. Before I came back home, I went to Old Friends in Lexington and met Silver Charm. That horse is probably my most favorite of all."

Adam smiled easily at her. "You will definitely get to meet him. He's stabled at Pimlico right now, so he's close."

After they had finished their pie, they made their way into the living room and sat on the couch by the fire. Julep jumped up on the couch and settled herself directly in between them.

"Looks like you have a little guard dog," Adam laughed.

"Is she okay on the couch? I'll move her if you'd like. I let her do whatever she wants at home – I love to spoil her," Macy said with a guilty grin.

"No, she's fine right where she is. Although I'd prefer to sit closer to you, but I don't want to disturb Her Highness," he joked, giving Julep a little pat.

Between the full meal, the bourbon, and the fire, Macy felt so warm inside, warm and *safe*. She liked that Adam naturally made her feel this way too.

Even though Julep was sitting in the middle, Adam laid his arm along the back of the couch and draped it over Macy's shoulder. With his fingers, he gently massaged her upper arm and shoulder, and then moved to the back of her neck. Macy leaned into his caresses, moaning quietly. It had been a long time since anyone had given her a massage.

Before she knew it, she and Adam were kissing again. He had reached over, tilted her chin towards him, and leaned in until their lips met. Macy gently pushed Julep to the floor, and the pup responded with an indignant glare at her mom before she curled up in front of the fire. Just like before, Macy climbed on top of Adam, straddling him with her legs, and holding his face to hers, her fingers in his hair.

They stayed like this for quite some time with Adam running his hands under Macy's sweater, unclasping her bra, and cupping her breasts in his hands. He lifted up her sweater and held one breast to his mouth, sucking on her nipple as Macy arched her back, pressing herself further into him. She had a feeling they would be getting close again, even though she knew in her heart she wasn't ready to be complicating her life this way.

"Would you like to go upstairs?" Adam asked breathlessly, hopefully.

Macy's head told her to stop, to grab her coat, and to leave immediately. Instead, she leaned forward, kissed Adam hard on the mouth, pulling away only slightly to whisper, "yes," in his ear.

~ Chapter 17 ~

"Merry Christmas!" Cora sang as Macy opened the front door early the next day. The two girls hugged in greeting as Tommy brought up the rear, arms loaded down with a large pile of presents.

"Merry Christmas, sis!" He said, his face wreathed in smiles. Christmas had always been Tommy's favorite holiday, and, as usual, he was decked out in his ugly Christmas sweater and Santa hat.

Inside the house was toasty warm with a fire roaring in the kitchen fireplace, and cinnamon buns were baking in the oven. There was just something about Christmas morning, everything felt different. The air was lighter, softer, and worries seemed to melt away under the embraces of family members and long-lasting holiday traditions.

Macy had woken up earlier in the morning in her own room. Her evening with Adam had taken an unexpected turn when she allowed him to take her to bed, but she had snuck out into the night, heavy with the pre-dawn darkness, and came home. He had not stirred as she slipped out of his bed and made her way down the stairs.

She wasn't sure how she felt about last night's tryst, but with her brother and sister-in-law here, Macy decided to focus on the here and now and think about Adam later.

"You ladies are in for a treat," Tommy said with a wicked grin. "Large plates of Tommy's Famous Omelets are coming right up!" And with that, he whipped out his ancient Christmas-themed apron, complete with the characters from Rudolph the Red-Nosed Reindeer, and got to work at the stove. Macy and Cora laughed at him as they set the table and poured cups of coffee and glasses of orange juice.

"Decaf for me, unfortunately," Cora said with a sad smile. "This baby can't get here soon enough. I need my caffeine back!"

"I thought you could have one cup of regular a day?" Macy asked.

"I can, and I do occasionally, but since I've been without it, even that one cup makes me all crazy and jittery. I figure it's best to just go without it if possible." She patted her slightly protruding belly. "Only five more months to go," she laughed. "Feels like forever!"

When Tommy finished with the omelets, the family of three sat down together to enjoy their Christmas breakfast. Eggs, bacon, toast, sausage, and cinnamon buns were piled high on their plates. Before they ate, Tommy said grace.

"Dear Lord. We thank you for this day and we thank you for allowing us to come together to celebrate your son's birthday. Lord, bless this food, our family, and please bless our mother who is with you today. Amen."

Macy's eyes glistened heavily with tears, but she refused to shed them. Her mother would not have wanted her to be unhappy today – not on Christmas Day. That was the first thought that had entered her mind when she awoke. Her mother would have wanted only happy smiles today.

"That was beautiful," Cora whispered. She, too, looked on the verge of tears, but took a deep breath and regained control.

"Mom would have wanted us to be happy today," Macy said simply. "She wouldn't want tears or sadness – not on Christmas." When Tommy nodded, she continued. "I feel her with us right now, you know? She's here in spirit, and then when she's done, she'll probably head out to the barn like she always did and feed special treats to the horses." Macy laughed softly to herself.

"Remember how she'd make stockings for all the horses and dogs?" Tommy asked.

"Yes, and we always teased her that their stockings were bigger than ours!"

"That's because they were!"

Macy and Tommy told Cora how they'd joke with their mother, saying that she loved her animals more than she loved her children. Of course, they knew it wasn't true, but it was a longstanding family joke. Hadley fiercely loved her kids, but her fur-kids had a special place in her heart as well. But Macy and Tommy hadn't minded – they were animal lovers too.

"I mean, I do love Hunter more than most people, so I get where mom was coming from." Macy said with a wink.

After breakfast, the three opened presents they had gotten for one another. Cora especially loved the baby outfits that Macy had purchased.

"They're perfect, Mace, thank you! I especially like this one with the fox print." She held up a tiny pair of pajamas, complete with hat, with frolicking red foxes printed all over.

Macy squealed when she opened an exquisite painting of Fitz. "This is amazing – who did this?" The artist had perfectly captured Fitz's dappled grey coloring, his soft features, and his kind eye.

"Remember my friend Charlie from high school? He does some portrait painting on the side. I know you have a similar painting of Hunter, so I figured you'd need one of your new steed. I snapped some pictures of him right after you brought him home and sent them to Charlie. He's painted quite a few horses before, so he was able to do this pretty quickly."

Macy stood up and hugged her brother tightly.

Tears were threatening to spill over again. “What a thoughtful gift. I love it so much,” she said as she hugged Cora next. “Now I have fancy paintings of my two best boys. What a wonderful gift.”

~~~~~

Later that evening, Macy sat in Molly’s parents’ living room with Molly and Erin. Everyone had enjoyed a fabulous Christmas dinner prepared by Karen and were full to the brim after dessert and coffee.

Rick, Beau, and Kevin had disappeared into the family room and were most likely falling asleep on the couch in front of the television. Karen was cleaning up the kitchen and insisted that everyone leave her to it. Erin had laughed at her mother as Karen had always been very particular about how she organized her kitchen. Too many people helping clean up stressed her out. It was just easier for her to do it herself, as she said.

Macy sighed happily as she held her mug of hot chocolate to her chest. She was so grateful to the Sorrensons for yet again opening their home to her on another holiday, and she told Molly and Erin just that.

“Will you stop with all that?” Erin said with grin. “You’re family, Mace, you’ve always been. We want you here, so don’t act like you’re putting us out.”

“What Erin said,” smiled Molly with a wink.

“But since you’re here,” Erin said with a wicked grin, “you’d better dish about last night. Molly told me you had dinner with Adam.”

“There’s really…not much to tell,” Macy stammered.

“Liar!” Shouted Molly. “You’re blushing!”

The three girls started laughing before Macy gave in. “Okay, okay, I’ll tell you.” She took a deep breath and
~~~~~

looked both happy and embarrassed. "He made me this beautiful dinner and we had wonderful conversation. He's...surprisingly easy to be with. I'm not sure why that didn't come across at first. And then after dessert, he, umm, gave me a tour of his bedroom," she finished up with a guilty grin.

"And did you enjoy yourself?" Erin asked.

"Yes, very much."

"Then that's all that matters," Erin said seriously. "Don't overthink it. Don't analyze anything. Just live in this moment. If crap hits the fan later on, worry about it then."

Macy nodded in agreement. Erin had such a realistic, easy perspective on life, and it made Macy jealous. She wished she could go with the flow and learn to enjoy her own life a bit more, but there were some days she just couldn't get out of her own head.

"What Erin said," Molly said with a laugh. "This is why I've always let my big sis do the talking – she usually gets it right."

"*Usually?* I think you meant, *always!*" Erin said, swatting at her sister. "So Mace, details. About the sex."

Macy's face reddened again. "You guys, I can't go into detail! But I will say this, he is…how should I put it…*very* experienced. Like, he knows exactly what to do. Mine you though – prior to him, it had been way too long since I'd last had sex, so I might not be the best judge."

"Are you saying he's the best you've ever had?" Erin asked.

Macy thought for a second. She thought about how Adam had taken her upstairs last night, how he'd undressed her tantalizing slow, so slow that she felt she was bursting out of her skin needing his touch. Then she thought about how he'd laid her down on his bed, spread her legs, and tasted her. Everything he did, every move he made was smooth, yet calculated. He had been a man on a mission, and she had happily gone right along with him.

"Earth to Mace!" Molly shouted, waving her hand in front of her friend's face. "I'd say that's probably a yes then!"

Macy shook her head to clear it. "Oh my goodness, you two are too much. But, yes, I'd say he's the best."

"Have you heard from him today?" Asked Erin.

"Yes, he sent me a text this morning and said Merry Christmas. He told me he'd like to stop by later if I got home early enough." Macy smiled to herself. "I think I'll tell him that I'm getting ready to leave if he'd still like to come over."

~~~~~

When Macy returned home later that evening, she decided to take a quick walk to the barn with Julep to check on the horses. They nickered their greetings as she entered the barn and flicked on the overhead lights. Both Hunter and Fitz blinked by the sudden brightness, and Macy laughed when she saw the pine shavings she used as stall bedding matted in Fitz's mane.

"Looks like someone had been down for the count. Did you have a nice nap?" She asked as she walked over to the horse, holding his head and planting a quick kiss on his nose. Fitz nudged her pockets and she giggled as she pulled out some peppermints. "You are already so spoiled," she said as she wrapped the mints, feeding them to both her boys.

As Julep ran around the barn searching for mice, Macy did a check to make sure both horses had plenty of hay and water. She noticed that Hunter's blanket had
~~~~~

slipped slightly, so she adjusted the buckles until it was snug once again.

Before she had left the Sorrensons', she had texted Adam, telling him she'd be home later if he wanted to stop by. He had responded almost immediately that he was leaving a friend's house and would be over shortly.

Finishing up with Hunter, Macy laid a hand on his well-muscled chestnut-colored neck. "Am I making a mistake getting involved with him?" She asked her horse, truly hoping that he could speak and offer some insight. "Erin had some pretty good advice for me tonight," she went on. "She told me that my Christmas present to myself should be to stop thinking so hard and worrying so much. To just live and be in the moment. To figure everything out as it comes along. While that would be great in theory, that's almost impossible for someone like me. If I could, I'd plan out every day for the next ten years of my life!" Macy laughed to herself, realizing how ridiculous that sounded. She needed to relax a little and let go. Just let life live itself.

The truth was, and Macy could hardly believe it, but Adam made her happy. She realized that she hadn't been in the best frame of mind when Adam had come knocking on her door after her mother's death, and she essentially opened fire on the first person to cross her. Yes, his asking to buy the property when he did was insensitive, but he truly hadn't meant anything by it. Now that she had gotten to know him, Macy realized that Adam had a good heart; he was a little rough and abrasive at times, but he meant well.

Macy had just walked into the house from the back door when the doorbell rang in the front.

"Hi," she said, greeting Adam with a smile. "Merry Christmas."

"Merry Christmas," he said with a shy smile. He walked in and hugged her tight. Macy closed her eyes and laid her head on his shoulder. She inhaled his scent, a mixture of horses, cologne, and whiskey.

"Did you have a nice time with the Petersons?" The Peterson family lived a few miles away, and Macy had gone to school with their oldest daughter, Francine. They rode too, were members of the Hunt Club, and had recently gotten into the racing business with Adam.

"I did. They have a lovely home. It was very kind of them to include me today. Did you have a good time with Molly's family?"

"Yes, I always do. The Sorrensons are the kindest people on earth."

"I need to get to know them better. I met Rick and Karen very briefly at the Hunt Ball, but that was it." Adam looked uncomfortable for a moment but went on. "So, I have a little something for you," he said, pulling a small yet brightly wrapped present out of his coat pocket.

"Oh no. We're not doing gifts. We're not there yet!" Macy exclaimed. "I didn't get you a single thing. I didn't even plan on seeing you today."

"It's nothing special, I promise. I just saw it the other day at the store and thought of you. Please," he said, pushing the gift towards her, "open it."

Macy sighed dramatically but took the gift and unwrapped it. Inside was an elegant business card holder with a foxhunting motif decorated on the outside. On the back was engraved the letter "M."

"I found it at one of the local antique shops. I know you like foxhunting décor, and when I picked it up and saw the M on the back, I figured it was a sign. I was meant to find it for you." Adam said, clearly proud of himself. "I know things have been rough for you with losing your mom and then leaving your job, but you're making a fresh start now and doing great. I thought you could put your new cards from Beau's practice in it."

Macy could not believe how incredibly thoughtful that was. Adam was right. Within a matter of weeks, she had lost almost everything she'd known, everything she'd come to rely on, for years. Her mom, who had been her rock and foundation, and her home and job in Kentucky, a place she had come to cherish. All of it was gone in what felt like a blink of an eye.

Overwhelmed by Adam's kindness and generosity, Macy was at a loss for words. Tears welled up in her eyes and then spilled over quickly, but she didn't even try and stop them. Instead she wrapped her arms around Adam's neck and pulled him into a tight hug.

"Thank you so much," she whispered in his ear. "It has been a rough few months, but I am starting fresh. Or, at least I'm trying to."

She pulled away slightly, met Adam's soft, concerned gaze, and brushed a piece of hair out of his eyes. He held her head in both hands and kissed her gently and slowly. He couldn't remember the last time he had felt such a strong emotional connection to a woman, but he also knew that Macy was feeling fragile today, the first Christmas without her mother. He stopped kissing her and pulled away.

Macy's eyes flickered open, and she shook her head a bit to clear it. "Would you like something to eat or drink? I have plenty of leftover cookies and fudge."

They made their way into the kitchen, Julep jumping at Adam's legs, trying to get his attention. He picked up the little dog and settled down in the breakfast nook while Macy put on the coffee pot. They had both agreed that a little cup would be the perfect way to cap off a wonderful Christmas.

"Any plans for New Year's?" Asked Adam,

blowing on his coffee before taking a sip.

"No plans. I'm not even sure what I'm doing tomorrow much less next week. No, wait, I'm on call tomorrow, so I might be working," she said, also blowing on her coffee to cool it down.

"I'm actually going to be in Middleburg, Virginia, for a few days, and I'd be very happy if you joined me. We could ring in the New Year together." He had such a hopeful look on his face that Macy hated herself for crushing it.

"I don't think that's such a good idea. I'm really enjoying spending time with you and getting to know you better, but I don't think we've progressed to the *going away together* phase just yet." She gave him a tiny smirk before continuing. "That's not to say that it doesn't sound fun. I adore Middleburg and haven't been there in years. Are you going for any particular reason?"

"Yes, I'll actually be there on both business and pleasure. I have some clients down there that I need to catch up with, and since I lived in the area for a while, I'm meeting up with some friends. One of them always has a huge party at his farm on New Year's Eve. I'm not much of a party person myself, but I actually look forward to this one. I'd certainly love to have you with me, even if it's just for the night."

"You just want to have someone to kiss on New Year's, that's all," she laughed. "I've figured you out."

Adam's eyes danced as he joked back. "Yep, you got me. I'd like to show my pretty new neighbor off to all my old buddies."

"Well, like I said, I can't seem to get my life together more than one day in advance, much less one week, but I'll let you know if I change my mind."

~ Chapter 18 ~

The week between Christmas and New Year's brought record low temperatures, which made everyone unhappy. Marylanders knew that late January and February could bring some frigid weather, but it was frustrating for it to be this cold in December.

Macy had just come back inside from doing her barn chores and was rubbing her hands together to try and get the blood flowing again. She had wanted to ride but had decided against it when the icy wind cut right through her, burning her lungs with every breath.

Work with Beau had picked up which was both good and bad. Macy was happy to be busy and have more to do, but it also meant that there were more horses falling ill. The dip in temperatures caused a lot of horses to colic, their sensitive bellies tying in knots for reasons still unknown to most. Beau had remarked just the day before how horses were the definition of a paradox. They were so big and strong and powerful, yet so vulnerable and fragile, taken down by what seemed to be the smallest things.

Since the business was growing though, Beau was just about ready to bring Macy on full-time, a change she was definitely looking forward to. Sometime in January, Macy would be a permanent member of Monkton Equine Medicine. She really liked the name, (it was Molly's idea), and was proud of how quickly Beau had grown his practice. He had only been in Maryland for just over a year and now he was a few weeks away from having two full-time veterinarians on call. For now, they were still doing farm calls, but eventually, as things progressed, Beau wanted to open up a clinic where they could house their patients and perform small surgeries. Macy couldn't wait to get back into the operating room.

She felt her cell phone buzz in her pocket and took it out to see a text message from Erin.

Can you give me a call when you can? I may need that room sooner than later.

Oh no, Macy thought. Poor Erin. Not wanting to spoil her Christmas, Macy hadn't asked her how things were that night. And Erin and Kevin both seemed okay, so Macy hadn't thought much of it.

Macy fixed herself a cup of regular coffee, added the French Vanilla creamer she liked, and sat down to give Erin a call. She answered immediately.

"Hey Mace, thanks for calling so quickly." Erin sounded incredibly tired.

"Of course. What's going on?"

"Just the usual. We've been at each other's throats for days now, and…" Erin broke off and Macy could hear a sob rising in her friend's throat. "Mace, I'm just done. I can't do it anymore. Were you serious about letting me come stay with you for a bit? If so, can I come tonight?"

"Erin, I'm *so* sorry you're going through all this. Yes, I was serious about the room – you know I'd love the company. Come now. Come whenever you'd like. I'm here."

Erin thanked Macy profusely, so grateful she was to have a friend she could turn to during this time. She could easily have gone to live with her sister, but Erin hadn't wanted to disrupt Molly's new life with Beau as the two were still newlyweds. Of course, Molly had offered the spare room to her sister, but she understood why Erin felt more comfortable living with Macy.

When they hung up, it was agreed that Erin would finish packing a few bags and would head to Macy's farm which was about forty minutes north of the city. In the meantime, Macy went up to prepare the spare bedroom for Erin's arrival. This room had been Tommy's growing up, but after he had gotten married, Hadley had turned it into a tastefully-decorated guest room. It had a jack and jill bathroom that connected on the other side to the fourth and final bedroom upstairs, a room that had been converted into an exercise room, complete with treadmill and stationary bike. Hadley hadn't used the equipment often as she preferred to take long walks outside, but she had taken the bike for a spin when the weather was exceptionally horrific.

Macy changed the sheets on the queen-sized bed and added fresh hand and bath towels in the bathroom. Finally, she replaced a burnt-out light-bulb in one of the lamps on the end tables so Erin would have plenty of light if she wanted to read or do some work while in bed.

As with the rest of the house, the room sported an equestrian flair, but it was subtle. The walls were painted a pale blue and two abstract horseracing paintings flanked each side of the bed. On the dresser sat an antique riding helmet and a pair of horseshoes had been hung over the doorway into the bathroom. The bed comforter was a navy, hunter green, and white tartan pattern; at the foot of the bed was a large wooden tack trunk that had been repurposed to hold extra pillows and blankets. *I hope Erin will be happy here*, Macy sighed. Her heart was breaking for her friend.

Downstairs Macy went to throw the makings for a delicious chicken noodle soup into the crock pot. *There's nothing better than some comfort food during times of crisis*. Shredded chicken, broth, carrots, potatoes, celery, onions, and some seasoning to spice things up. She'd add in the noodles about a half hour before it was to be done. Soon the house would smell warm and inviting, perfect for Erin's homecoming on this cold, dreary late December day.

Macy had just finished evening feeding at the barn and walked through the back door when Erin knocked on the front. Julep gave a little howl and scurried to the door, anxious to see who was visiting.

When Macy opened the front door and saw Erin standing on the porch, luggage in hand with tears streaming down her face, she reached out and quickly embraced her friend, pulling her in for a tight hug.

"Oh Erin," Macy said, holding her friend and rubbing her back gently while Erin cried into her shoulder. "I'm so sorry about all this. I can't imagine how you must be feeling." She wrapped her arm around Erin's shoulders and led her inside. "Here, let's go inside where it's warm. Your tears are going to freeze on your cheeks!"

Macy led Erin to the overstuffed armchair in the family room, wrapped her in a thick blanket, and brought her a steaming mug of chamomile tea. Julep, sensing her friend was distraught, curled up on Erin's lap and licked her face.

Erin laughed softly at the sweet little dog. "Thanks, Julep. I feel better already." She placed her tea on the end table next to the chair and held the dog tightly with both arms wrapped around her. Julep snuggled close, curling in a tight ball in Erin's lap.

Erin looked up at Macy who walked in with her own mug of tea. "I'm stealing your dog. Sorry in advance."

"I'm pretty attached to her – how about we share?" Macy said with a wink. She, too, had held Julep in her arms many nights as she cried herself to sleep. She would still wake up randomly, shaking from a nightmare, only to realize that the nightmare was real. Her mom had indeed died. Macy didn't know what she would have done without Julep's presence.

"Deal – joint custody of Julep it is. Thanks for the tea, by the way, it's just what I needed."

"You're welcome. You take it the same way your sister does."

Erin laughed. "I guess you've been wiping the tears of the Sorrenson girls for quite some time now, huh?"

"Just returning favors. Those Sorrenson girls have been pretty good to me too over all these years."

"Well, you are doing one hell of a favor for me right now, and I want you to know how much I appreciate it."

"Don't even think about it. You're doing *me* a favor. I told you, Julep and I are a little lonely here, and I'm still not myself after everything that's happened. Having another person around will make me feel, I don't know, normal. Like, I'll be able to have regular conversations with you instead of my dog. No offense, Julep." The little dog shot her mother a look that said, *well, thanks a lot!*

"I can't believe it's here. The day I separated from my husband."

"So what happened? You guys seemed okay on Christmas."

"We had basically agreed to a cease-fire, if you will, for the holiday. We saw his family in the morning and then mine in the evening. Neither side knows anything yet, although I bet Kevin will call his parents soon."

"And you haven't told your parents yet?"

Erin shook her head. "No. I figured I'd settle in here and then go talk to them tomorrow or the next day. They deserve to know what's going on. I feel bad having kept this from them, but I honestly thought it was just a rough patch that would blow over."

"I would have done the same exact thing. No sense worrying them if it's something you could work out without getting everyone involved."

"We have been fighting for, goodness, so long at this point. I don't remember the last time we were happy. But, Mace, it's all my fault. I'm a fraud. He made a vow to me under the condition that one day we'd have a family. And I took that away from him." She started to cry again.

"Erin, stop crying. Listen to me. This is *not* your fault! You've been married for what, seven years now?" Erin nodded. "Seven years is a long time. How on earth are you supposed to know what you're going to what in life seven years later? People change drastically in the span of just a year or two. I'm going to tell you what you've been telling me for months – you need to cut yourself some slack. When you got married, you probably truly thought you'd want a family with Kevin. But things changed. Life happened, and you decided that motherhood wasn't for you – and that's *okay*."

"I know, and you're right. But I can't stop beating myself up over it. We'd still be together if I'd just give him a kid. *One* kid. But I just can't do it. And you know what I kept saying? I would ask him, Kevin, why am I not enough? When did I stop being enough for you?" Tears steamed silently down Erin's cheeks. "I kept trying to make it about me when it was really about him and what I took away from him."

"No, Erin, stop. You did not take anything away from him. You decided that you needed to do what was best for you – to make a decision for *you*. Having a child is huge and life-changing, and you decided that it wasn't what you wanted. I know it's hard now and everything's still so fresh, but one day you'll see that you made the right decision. It's never wrong to put yourself first, especially in a situation like this."

The two talked long into the night, stopping only to eat large, steaming bowls of chicken noodle soup. Then Erin went outside with Macy as she did the night check on the horses.

"Ahh I've missed this, having horses just steps from the house," Erin said as she slid open the barn doors and inhaled the sweet scent of horse. "I've missed this smell too. I don't get to mom's nearly enough to visit. I've been a terrible mom to Ruby."

Ruby was Erin's retired event horse. She was in her mid-twenties now and enjoying the easy life at her parents' farm.

"Is she still sound enough to ride?"

"She is, lightly though," Erin answered. "I took her out a few times over the summer, just light hacks with Molly on Traveller. It's nice to get the old guys out once in a while, but we have to watch them. When they get together, they forget they are senior citizens and want to run! We let them out into a quick canter, but that's it. Anymore would be way too much for them, especially Ruby."

"You know what I've learned," Macy said as she tossed a large flake of hay to Hunter and Erin threw a large flake into Fitz's stall. "I've learned that new beginnings call for new horses!" Macy laughed to herself as she began to rationalize this thought to Erin. "After my mom passed and I went back to Kentucky, I ended up quitting my job and coming home with Fitz. It was the end of one chapter, and it only seemed right to christen the beginning of a new one with a new family member. Well, two family members," she corrected herself as Julep zoomed by on the hunt for a mouse. "And when

Molly thought things were over between she and Beau, she came back to Maryland with Gypsy in tow!"

"You're right, and it's funny you mention that," Erin said as she let herself into Fitz's stall and hugged the grey horse on the neck. "As I was driving up here, I actually thought to myself that getting a new horse would be a great distraction. I wanted to get back into training and competing, and now seems like as good of a time as any."

"I agree completely!" Macy enthused. "I know your job keeps you busy, but you'll still have plenty of time to devote to a new horse. I'm assuming you'll want another Thoroughbred?"

"Oh yeah, no question about that. They are the best…sorry Hunter." The big Warmblood looked at her softly letting her know he took no offense.

"Let me know when you're ready to start looking and I'll talk to Adam. I'm sure he knows plenty that are transitioning out of racing and in need of a second career."

"I'm actually ready now, so please talk to him when you can. And speaking of, how are things with you two?"

Macy told Erin that things were going well, but she was hoping to take it all very slow.

"He asked me to go to Middleburg with him for New Year's, but I'm not sure I'm ready to go away with him yet. I mean, it wasn't that long ago that I was still hating his guts."

"Oh my goodness, Mace, I'm terrible. Here you are starting a new relationship and I come bursting in your door and setting up shop. Just say the word and I'm out of here – I don't want it to turn into Three's Company around here!"

"Erin! Absolutely not – you are not getting in the

way or interrupting anything! I want to take things slow. Slower than slow."

"Are you sure? Because I am capable of getting my own place. I just thought it would seem less…I don't know…less *real* if I stayed with someone for a bit. I guess in my mind getting an apartment makes it feel more formal, like my marriage is officially over. If I stay with you or Molly, then it feels temporary. Like one day I'll wake up and Kevin will call me and say, come home, babe, everything's going to be okay."

"I completely understand how you feel. I truly do. And trust me when I say this, you are more than welcome to stay here for as long as you like. One week, one year, I don't care. I live in this big empty house all alone, and I really could use some company. Like I said, you're doing me a favor too."

The two girls embraced with Erin vowing to be the best house guest Macy ever had.

"I believe you will be. As long as you don't steal Julep, that is." Macy gave Erin a sly smile as she turned off the barn lights and made her way to the house.

Erin grinned back at her. "I can't make any promises where Julep is concerned."

~ Chapter 19 ~

It was New Year's Eve, and the local liquor store was bustling. Macy stood in line with her arms full of alcohol, and had it not been a holiday, she probably would have felt like a lush. Since she only drank socially, she had virtually nothing in the house to ring in the New Year with. Macy had invited Molly over to celebrate with her and Erin. Beau was on call that night, so he figured he would turn in early and get as much sleep as possible before any calls came through.

Once Macy made it to the counter, she sat down her red wine and champagne selections and started rooting through her handbag for her wallet.

"Looks like someone is having a party tonight," came a sweet voice from behind. Macy turned to see Mrs. Evans, a member of the Hunt Club who owned a farm two roads over from Macy.

"Mrs. Evans, it's so good to see you!" Macy said with a bright smile, hugging the elderly woman. "And yes, I'm kind of having a party – just Molly and Erin."

"Good for you, dear. I'm happy to see you doing so well." Mrs. Evans, while a bit older than Hadley, had been a good friend to the family for years. She had been devastated to learn of her good friend's passing and had brought casserole after casserole to Macy after the tragedy.

The two caught up briefly, recapping their Christmases and plans for the New Year. Mrs. Evans was having some friends over that evening as well, most of whom Macy knew from the club.

"After the party tonight, it's clean up tomorrow, and then we're heading south like always." Mrs. Evans and her husband, Edward, were snowbirds and owned a house in Boca Raton, Florida. Every year they fled the bitter cold in early January and didn't return until April. Macy thought how nice it would be to escape the Maryland winters year after year, to feel the warm sun on your face, to take regular walks on the beach and dips in the ocean.

"I'm going to be a snowbird one day, just like you. You and Mr. Evans are the smart ones!" Macy laughed.

"We started doing it fifteen years ago and it was the best decision we've ever made. Of course, we miss the majority of hunting season, but oh well. My old bones can't take the cold like they used to. And speaking of old, missy, you're not getting any younger these days. When are you going to find yourself a man and settle down?"

Coming from anyone other than Mrs. Evans, who was known for her quick wit, this would have been insulting, but Macy knew she only wanted the best for her.

Laughing out loud, Macy responded, shaking her head, "Oh Mrs. Evans, you certainly don't mince words. Now that I'm feeling a bit better, I'm on the lookout. I'm not looking too hard, but I *am* looking."

"What about that neighbor of yours, Adam Cleary? He's easy on the eyes – and he's walking distance from your house. It doesn't get more convenient than that."

Macy stammered for a moment, wondering if Mrs. Evans knew more than she was letting on, but how could she?

"Um...Adam? Well, yeah, he is very nice. But I, uh, hardly know him," Macy replied, unable to look Mrs. Evans in the eye.

"Well there's no time like the present to change that," she said with a wink. "On that note, I'm off. It was great to see you, dear, and please, even though we'll be in Florida, don't hesitate to call should you need us."

~~~~~

"There's no way she could have known," Erin said, shaking her head. "Adam is the new bachelor in town, so that's probably why he came to mind."

Macy, in the kitchen preparing dinner for the girls, had filled Molly and Erin in on her earlier conversation with Mrs. Evans. Erin was setting the table, and with the fine china at that, while Molly concocted a béarnaise sauce for the filet mignons Macy had in the oven. Even though the girls had decided to stay in for the holiday, they still wanted to have a fancy dinner.

"Would it bother you if people found out you two are dating?" Molly asked, stirring the delicious sauce.

"See that's the thing," Macy responded as she washed the fresh asparagus they would also be enjoying. "I don't think we're dating. We're just, I don't know, fooling around." She stopped what she was doing and looked at her two friends. "Honestly, I enjoy spending time with him, but Adam is more of a distraction for me at this point. I still have absolutely no clue what I want out of whatever it is we're doing. Does that make me a bad person?"

"Of course not," answered Erin, who had begun laying out the silverware at each place setting. "You two are grown adults, and it's not like you've made any promises to each other. If being friends with benefits with your next door neighbor is what you need right now, go for it."

The girls laughed at Erin's candor. Talking everything out with Molly and Erin always made her feel better, but Macy had to admit that her run-in with Mrs.
~~~~~

Evans had upset her. Not because she may have known about her and Adam, but because it was forcing her to think about what it is exactly they were doing.

"What do you think Adam wants out of all of this?" Macy asked seriously. "We haven't discussed anything, nor do I really want to. We've only been hanging out for a few weeks now."

"He's probably in the same boat you are," Molly reasoned. "He's divorced, he's new to the area, and he knows you are going through a tough time. I bet he's content with playing things by ear."

Macy sighed. "I hope so. Because if he wants to get serious, then I'm out. And while I don't think that's what he wants, his inviting me to Middleburg for the New Year definitely threw me off."

"I wouldn't read too much into it. If he had invited you on a week-long vacation to the islands, that would be one thing. But this was technically just a holiday function where he asked you to be his plus one," Molly reasoned. She tried to downplay everything with Adam so Macy wouldn't get herself too riled up just yet. "Okay, the béarnaise sauce is ready!"

As the girls sat down to their fancy dinner, they switched gears a bit and talked about the upcoming year.

Macy gave a heavy sigh as she buttered her baked potato. "I'll be glad to put this year behind me. It was definitely the worst of my entire life." She glanced over at Erin. "I know you didn't lose your mother, but I know you can relate."

"Oh yes I certainly can," Erin said with a sad smile. She had broken the news about her separation to her parents the day before, and while they were devastated for Erin, they supported her completely. But now that that task was done, everything seemed so real. Sometime next year, unless she or Kevin had a drastic change of heart, Erin would be a divorcee.

"At least Molly had a good year," Macy said with a smile as she reached across and took her best friend's hand. "I still can't get over how beautiful you looked on your wedding day."

"Thanks, love," Molly said happily. "It's hard to believe so much has happened since then. August really wasn't that long ago."

"Does anyone have any New Year's resolutions? Or just something they want to accomplish? Molly, what's the status with your latest book?" Erin asked as she topped off everyone's glass with the merlot Macy had purchased earlier today.

"It's almost done," Molly said after she had taken a sip of the delightful red wine. "I am in the final stages of writing, then I'll send to my copyeditor and go from there. It should be ready for publication by late spring, I think."

"What's this one called?" Macy asked.

"It's still untitled!" Molly groaned. "Nothing seems to stick. And, honestly, I love this story, but I don't think anything I'll ever do will top *Lexington,*" she sighed. Molly wrote *Lexington: A Novel*, when she was living with Macy in Kentucky two summers ago. It was there among the bluegrass that Molly met Beau, fell madly in love, but also, briefly, had her heart broken.

But that heartbreak led her to Gypsy and led both back to Maryland where Beau followed shortly thereafter. It was a dramatic season in Molly's life, but one she'd always cherish. *Lexington*, as a result, had been Molly's best-selling novel to date.

"Not true," said Macy, shaking her head at Molly. "Every book you have written and will write in the future will be a success. I just think *Lexington* will always be special to you because that's what you were working on when you met Beau…and Gypsy!"

"Yes!" Laughed Erin. "The way you drool over that horse, I can't tell which one you love more!" She said with a wink. Of course she loved Beau best, but it was hard not to fall head over heels for Gypsy too. The horse was cuddly and affectionate, an absolute sweetheart.

"Ha, Erin, very funny," Molly said sarcastically but with a smile. "Just wait until you fall in love with your new horse. You won't know what hit you! And speaking of, it's your turn. What are you plans for the New Year? I'm assuming the new horse will be a big part of it."

For a moment, Erin looked wistful, her eyes taking on a faraway gleam, but she gathered herself quickly. "Yes, new horse for starters. Mace is going to talk to Adam to see if he has any racers who are retiring. Other than that, I'm not too sure. If Kevin and I are definitely heading for divorce, then I'll have to find a place to live at some point." When Macy started to protest, Erin quickly interjected. "You don't have to say it, Mace, I know I'm welcome here. And trust me, I'm going to take advantage of you for longer than I should! But I'm going to have to move on eventually. So maybe that's it for the year. New horse. New house."

"I absolutely won't hear of it. You two officially divorcing has nothing to do with you living here or finding your own place. I want a roommate damnit! You're staying!" Macy shouted, grinning broadly and pounding her fist on the table for emphasis.

"Don't argue with her, Erin," Molly wisely stated. "You'll never win. I know from experience."

"Well I guess we'll cross that bridge when we come to it," Erin said with a small smile. "Okay, Mace, your turn. What does the New Year look like for you?"

"First, I'm excited to be working full-time with Beau and growing the practice! Second, I can't wait until Fitz is healed. I really want to foxhunt with him next fall and winter. Finally, I want to…well…find the old Macy again. The one who didn't have to put so much effort and thought into life."

Molly reached over and grabbed her friend's hand. "You'll get there, my love. I promise."

"I know," Macy responded. "I'm just tired of not feeling myself. But having you two around, working more, and being with the horses, well, all of that will bring me home again."

"Us and Adam!" Erin blurted out.

"Ha! We'll see about that!" Macy said with a wicked grin.

And with that, the three girls raised their wine glasses in a toast. A toast to their friendship, their love for each other, and new beginnings.

~~~~~

"5! 4! 3! 2! 1! Happy New Year!!!" Erin shouted as they watched the ball drop in Times Square. They were thankful to usher in the New Year in the warmth and comfort of Macy's home, not in freezing New York City.

The three girls, giggly from way too much wine, all embraced tightly.

"Here's to a New Year! A fresh chapter!" Macy shouted, spilling a little of her wine on the wood floor. "Oh shit. Let me grab some paper towels."

At that moment, there was a knock on the door.

"I'll get it!" Molly said, rushing to the front of the house. She had an idea of who might be stopping by.

Molly led Beau in just as Macy finished cleaning
~~~~~

the wine off the floor.

"Happy New Year, brother!" Erin shouted, unsteadily walking over to give her brother-in-law a hug.

"Oh goodness," Beau laughed, shaking his head. "What have I walked in on? Looks like the three of you have been celebrating for quite some time."

Molly dissolved into giggles. What a sight they must all be to poor Beau who ended up working all night.

As they took turns wishing Beau a Happy New Year, Erin and Molly's parents called. Erin put them on speaker so everyone could hear them.

"Mom!!!" Erin sang. "Mom and Dad, we're a little drunk, but Haaaaappy New Yearrrr!" Everyone started laughing as this scene unfolded.

Macy, cradling Julep in her arms, was so thankful to be surrounded by friends who were truly family, but her heart ached. If only Hadley were around to call and wish her "Godspeed," as she always did each New Year. Macy hadn't realized, but this would be the first year she would live without her mom. Last year, even though her mom had passed, they had lived a portion of it together. This year, Macy was going it alone.

As if on cue, Tommy called in. "Happy New Year, sis!" He sounded like he had enjoyed quite a few beverages himself.

The two spoke while the Sorrenson girls and Beau finished their call with Karen and Rick. Cora hopped on the phone as well and reminded Macy that this was the year she'd become an aunt. She couldn't wait!

Shortly thereafter, Macy received another call, and this one was surprising.

"Adam?" She asked as she answered. She hadn't expected to hear from him.

"Happy New Year, Macy. I'm sorry we couldn't spend it together."

"It's okay," she said, slurring a bit. "The girls are here. I wasn't alone."

Adam laughed. "I can tell. Sounds like you ladies had quite the party."

"They had a great sale at the liquor store. Never realized I was such a fan of merlot."

She could hear Adam smile at the other end of the phone, and in that moment, her heart gave a small lurch. She missed him. Even though she hadn't wanted to go with him to the party in Middleburg, she had missed being with him.

"I'm actually glad you called," Macy said matter-of-factly. "Erin wants a new horse. Got any ready to retire? She likes mares." Macy, realizing she was sounding like an idiot, shook her head attempting to clear it.

"I do. I have a few that are being retired as we speak, and another two that will most likely be retired. Waiting to hear the final word from their owners. If you guys are around tomorrow, bring Erin by the track, and I'll show her what we have."

"It's a date."

~ Chapter 20 ~

There's just something about New Year's Day. The beginning of a new year, a fresh start. It feels as if anything is possible, like the world is your oyster, there for the taking.

The three girls woke around nine o'clock that next morning, relatively late for them. Macy, Julep galloping alongside, walked down to the barn to feed breakfast. It was a perfect winter day; the wind had died down, and the sun shining brightly made it feel warmer than it actually was. Even though she had a slight headache, Macy had a spring in her step and was humming softly to herself as she opened the barn doors wide.

She was greeted by a duet of angry whinnies.

"I know, I know. I'm late. I'm sorry!" Into the tack room, which doubled as the feed room, she grabbed their scoops, already filled with grain that had been portioned out the night before.

"How can two horses make so much noise?" She laughed to herself as she filled Hunter's bucket, then Fitz's. "And happy racehorse birthday to you, Fitz!" All thoroughbreds, regardless of their actual birthdays, celebrated New Year's Day as an unofficial birthday. This made entering races less of a headache. For example, that meant that all two year olds turned three on New Year's Day, even if they were actually born in March, and eligible for all three year old races.

Macy busied herself with mucking stalls and then opened Hunter's stall door into the dry lot so he could go in and out during the day. She filled water buckets, silently thanking herself for finally buying some heated ones, and threw multiple flakes of hay to each horse. With a final check that everything was in order, she blew them two kisses each and headed into the house.

The aroma of freshly-brewed coffee and frying bacon filled the house, and Macy inhaled deeply as she took off her boots in the mudroom.

"Something smells delicious," she said as she walked into the kitchen.

Both Molly and Erin were up, though still in their pajamas, and were hard at work preparing a hearty breakfast.

"For you, Madame," said Erin as she handed Macy a large mug of coffee. "I put the creamer on the table."

"Thank you," Macy said gratefully, clutching the mug tightly as she carried it over to the table. She loved her morning coffee, and with a bit of flavored creamer, it was perfection. "What can I do to help?"

"Not a thing," said Molly, who was flipping the bacon, allowing it to crisp evenly on both sides. "The eggs are almost done, and the bacon and sausage need two more minutes. Erin, are you done with the fruit?"

"Sure am." Erin walked over to the table, which was already set, with a bowl of fruit, sliced and ready to be enjoyed.

"Thanks! A girl could get used to this kind of service," Macy said.

"You can thank Molly," Erin said. "She had already started everything when I wandered in."

"First, we need to start the New Year off correctly – and that's with a big, delicious breakfast," reasoned Molly. "And second, Erin, you can't go looking for your new horse, a potential life-long partner, on an empty stomach, so eat up!"

As the girls dove into their breakfast, they laughed at their shenanigans from the night before. While each felt a bit of a headache, none of them were truly hungover.

"Beau called this morning and asked how I was feeling. I said, I feel fine, why do you ask? He said, 'Darlin' you were awfully drunk last night. I've never heard you repeat yourself so many times!'"

"You do repeat yourself when you get drunk, or even a little tipsy," smiled Erin. The sisters laughed at each other.

"So, ready for today?" Macy asked Erin. They were meeting Adam at Pimlico at noon. He had three horses who were getting ready to be retired, and he said Erin could have her pick.

Erin smiled genuinely. "I absolutely am. I should have gotten a new horse last year, but I let you-know-who talk me out of it. Never again will I let someone tell me what I can and cannot do."

"That's a girl!" Molly patted her sister on her back. "Hopefully one of them today tickles your fancy. New year, new horse, new attitude!"

The three laughed – maybe Molly was still a little drunk.

~~~~~

Macy hadn't been to Pimlico racetrack in years, but as they drove around, attempting to follow the instructions Adam gave, she couldn't help but get goosebumps when she saw the big golden galloping horses adorning the side of the grandstand. Places like this, that have seen so much history, that have meant so much to so many people, always gave Macy chills.

As they made their way to the backside, they were greeted by rows and rows of stables, all shedrow style, which is typical at a track. As they parked, Macy sent Adam a text letting him know they had arrived.
~~~~~

The three girls climbed out of Erin's black Range Rover, ("One of our last recent purchases together," she had said. "And I'm not giving it back!"), and were soon met by Adam, walking easily towards them with one gloved hand in his pocket and the other holding a coffee cup. He looked very handsome in his jeans, paddock boots, and Barbour coat.

"Good morning, ladies," he said with a wide smile. "Happy New Year. How's everyone holding up after last night?" He asked, grinning mischievously.

"We were not that drunk," Macy said.

"Are you sure about that?" he laughed, walking over to Macy and giving her a quick hug. Then he turned to the Sorrenson sisters. "I'm Adam," he said, extending his hand. "I don't believe we've formally met."

"Molly," she said, shaking his hand firmly. "I saw you at the Hunt Ball."

"But we were warned to stay away from you," Erin said with a wicked smile as she walked over and shook Adam's hand as well. "You were still the evil neighbor at that point."

"Thanks for that, Erin," Macy laughed. While you never knew what was going to come out of Erin's mouth, her quick remarks usually lightened the mood.

"Alright, Erin, I have three horses for you to see today. Two mares and a gelding."

"Perfect," said Molly. "Erin is a mare person."

"It's true," Erin agreed. "I love them. The feistier, the better."

"Well, you're in luck. Wait until you meet Jazzy. Not only is she a mare, but she's a redhead." Adam said.

Mares are notorious for being harder to work with than geldings, a male horse that's been gelded and is no longer a stallion. Redhead is a term warmly used to describe a horse chestnut in color. The horse world has a long-standing joke about redheads being more difficult than other colors. A chestnut mare can be a thing to watch out for!

"Excellent! I've always wanted my own version of Ginger from *Black Beauty*," said Erin. "I love a hot-head."

"It takes one to know one," Macy said affectionately as she wrapped her arm around Erin's shoulders. The three girls laughed as Adam turned to lead the way.

At the end of the barn stood a tall, solidly-built dark bay gelding. He didn't have a single white mark on him. As soon as he heard visitors, he pulled himself away from his hay net, and turned to greet his visitors.

"This here is Sampson, race name Sampson Hill. He'll be five, officially, in March. He was a pretty respectable racer, won us quite a bit, but he's just past his peak and ready for something new. He'll retire sound, all of them I'll show you today will, and would be up for any challenge. He's not the bravest, but he's willing, so he can probably be talked into just about anything. He's also the tallest of the ones you'll see today – he's 16.3 and, clearly, all muscle."

Sampson, by Thoroughbred standards, was a hefty boy. He looked like the incredible hulk. But he was friendly and interested in his visitors, and he stood sweetly as all three girls descended upon him.

"He's a little bulkier than I like them," noted Erin, "but he's a sweetheart."

"That he is; he definitely likes to be cuddled. And I'd say he's probably the barn favorite. Everyone's going to miss him."

Erin went into the stall to get a closer look at the horse. She ran her hands down his legs. "His legs look remarkably well for a coming five year old. How many times did he race?"

"Thirty-two, I believe. And he ran as a two year old. I can bring him out and put him on the lunge line if you'd like to see him go. I can't let you ride any of them due to legal purposes, but all three will be coming to my place within a few days, if they're not adopted before that, so you'll be able to ride then if you'd like. If you see one in particular you're really interested in, I can ship him or her out even sooner."

"Yes, I'd definitely want to ride before making up my mind."

They moved into the next barn and in the first stall was a very dark dappled grey, Molly's favorite. "Oh my goodness, Erin! Look at this little love!"

"This is Lighter, race name, Lights Above. She is coming four in February and didn't race as a two year old. She only raced six times, and it is just clear as day that she doesn't want to be a racehorse. Her only issue is that she's very timid, so she'd have to have a very advanced, brave rider, which it sounds like you are. I would imagine the right rider will go far with her. She's only 15.2 hands, but, like I said, she's still technically two."

"What a snuggle bug you are," cooed Macy as Lighter laid her head against Macy's chest. Erin had gone inside the stall to get yet another look.

"She's classic Thoroughbred," Erin remarked. Lighter was long and lean and leggy. With her dark dapples and ebony mane and tail, she was breathtaking.

"What do you think of her?" Molly asked.

"I think she's gorgeous. And I think I'm going to have a very tough decision to make!"

"Well, they're all coming home with me, so you can ride each one and take your pick," commented Adam. "I haven't made any other calls because I want you to have first choice, but I do have a handful of people looking. So you don't have to feel bad about the ones you don't take – they'll still get great homes. I'm very picky about where my horses end up."

At that, Macy smiled up at Adam, and he gave her a quick wink. Not all trainers took such great care of their horses, so it meant a lot to Macy to hear those words.

They moved halfway down the barn and stopped in front of a stall that appeared deserted. When all the other horses heard the sound of humans talking, they peered out, curiosity and the hope of peppermints taking over. But not at this stall.

"This is the redhead I was telling you about, Jazzy, race name Getjazzywithit." The group looked into the stall and were greeted with the sight of Jazzy's rump. "Hey, Jazz," called Adam. "Can her highness spare a moment? I'd like you to meet some friends." He put his hand into his coat pocket and crinkled the plastic wrapper of a peppermint. Jazzy, at the thought of treats, finally turned around.

"Knew that would do the trick," said Adam as he fed her a few peppermints. "Let me bring her out. She'll just turn right back around if I don't." He continued to talk about Jazzy's accomplishments as he grabbed her halter and lead. "Jazzy is coming five in April, did not race as a two year old. I think she's raced eighteen times. She's being retired because, while she loves her job, she just isn't putting up reasonable enough fractions anymore, and I'm not dropping her into the claimers."

Molly opened the latch to her door, and Adam led out the beautiful mare. "She's 16 hands even and may top out another inch or so. If you're looking for an eventing mount or a foxhunter, this is your girl. She's the bravest one I have in my barn and is a work horse. Unlike most mares, she'll give her all every time out. Her only issue, however, is she's not the sweetest."

As if to demonstrate his point, Jazzy pinned her ears back and gave her head a little shake. It was obvious that she wanted to get back to her hay.

"Oh look at you, you wicked little woman," Erin said, her eyes dancing. "You look like you're pretty darn rotten."

Adam laughed. "She does like to get into trouble. She'll turn over wheelbarrows, throw her brushes out of the caddy. If it's in reach, she'll try to destroy it. She'll pin her ears and make 'the mare face,' as I call it, but she doesn't bite or kick. Very respectful of your space. But if you're looking for one you can hug on and cuddle, she's not your girl."

"I'm not too cuddly myself these days," said Erin. She was giving the horse a serious once-over, feeling legs, picking up hooves, looking into her mouth. All the while Jazzy, while compliant, gave her a once-over herself, never taking her eyes off of Erin. "I like her build. She's a good medium. Not as wide as Sampson and not as dainty as Lighter. I like her. Can I see her lunge?"

"Absolutely," Adam said with a grin. He knew once Erin saw Jazzy move, it would seal the deal.

With Jazzy in tow, the four walked towards the round pen just outside the stable area. Adam attached the lunge line to her halter, grabbed the lunge whip in his right hand, and asked Jazzy to move out, walking briskly around the perimeter of the pen. Her gait was nice and even, and Erin could tell immediately that she was as smooth as silk.

When she moved into the trot, Adam heard a collectively gasp from the three friends. Jazzy's trot was everything you could ask for: forward, floaty, and strong.

"She'll be a great eventer," Macy whispered. "With that trot, she'll ace dressage and put you in good standing from the start." Erin just grinned back. She felt like a kid in a candy store.

Jazzy's canter was just as gorgeous as her trot, and Erin also liked the mare's willingness. As soon as they had entered the round pen, Jazzy had focused on Adam, waiting for his commands. She knew that it was time for work.

After she had been lunged in both directions, Adam pulled the mare up and gave her a loving pat on her neck. "What do you think?" He asked with a big smile.

"I think I've just found my next horse!"

~ Chapter 21 ~

Later that evening, Macy and Erin were relaxing in the living room when Macy's phone buzzed, signifying a text.

"Adam says that Jazzy is home and to let him know what time you'd like to ride her tomorrow."

"Will do. If I like her, I'll have her vetted, and then she'll be mine. I can't believe I'm really doing this. I'm getting a new horse. I feel like she's officially the start of a new chapter in my life."

"I know exactly what you mean. When I returned to Lexington after losing my mom, I couldn't see straight much less think anything through. And then the next thing I know, I'm saving Fitz and quitting my job. Fitz is that for me – a representation of my new life. I really am so happy to be home, but I still can't believe my mom is truly gone. She would have loved tagging along horse shopping today."

"And she would have loved meeting Etch A Sketch. What an absolutely gorgeous animal. How cool that he's heading into the Derby preps soon."

After he had put Jazzy away, Adam had showed the girls Etch, his big horse. A striking chestnut with a small stripe running down the length of his face, he reminded everyone a little of Secretariat. Macy had never seen a more handsome fellow.

The girls talked for a bit more before Erin retired to her bedroom. "Well, off to bed for me, I'm exhausted. I'll text Adam first though to figure out a time to see Jazzy tomorrow. Will you come watch us?"

"I wouldn't miss it." Macy said with a sincere smile. She was so happy that Erin seemed to be okay and moving on with her life. Last year had brought so many unwanted changes for her family and friends.

As Macy cleaned up the kitchen a bit, emptied and reloaded the dishwasher, and wiped down the counters, her phone buzzed again with a text message. It was Adam again, and he was asking her to come over.

While she did want to see him – she felt like they hadn't really spoken in days – she wasn't in the best of moods. The last few days had been jam-packed with holiday celebrations, and while she had been grateful for the distractions at the time, now, with everything over, she was just plain sad.

Macy: I probably shouldn't. I don't think I'd be the best company right now.
Adam: Post-holiday blues hitting you?
Macy: Something like that.
Adam: Come over for just a few. I'll make some tea. I just miss you.
Macy: You saw me a few hours ago!
Adam: I know – see what you've already done to me?

Macy smiled to herself as she texted back that she'd be over in a few.

~~~~~

"Thanks for coming," Adam said as he ushered Macy into the house. He had a fire going in the living room which tossed a soft glow over the room, and the whole house felt toasty warm.

"Where's our friend Miss Julep?" He asked as he took Macy's coat and hung it in the entryway closet.

"Fast asleep in bed with Erin. My dog's thrown me over for the new girl," she said with a smile. When she had knocked on Erin's door to tell her she was going
~~~~~

next door for a visit, Julep ran through and jumped on Erin's bed, circled around a few times, and then laid down with a contented sigh.

"Speaking of the new girl, I knew she'd go for Jazzy. I can't wait to see what those two end up doing together. You said Erin's an eventer, right?"

"Yes, she was pretty big time into it back in high school and college. She got out of it, mostly, during law school though. She just didn't have the time, and her mare, Ruby, was slowing down anyway. But I know she was regularly showing Prelim, and she may have even done one or two Intermediates. She's one of the best riders I've ever seen. She's completely fearless."

"I think Jazzy will be perfect for her. She'll be a challenge, no doubt about it, but nothing that Erin won't be able to handle."

"I'm sure she'll enjoy it!"

As they chatted more about Jazzy and the other horses' retirement, Adam took Macy's hand and led her back to the small country kitchen. The kitchen was located at the back of the house and had large windows that displayed a beautiful view into the backyard and fenced pastured beyond. Since it was dark, none of that could be seen, but Macy had been in this house multiple times when it was owned by Mrs. Radnor, the previous owner.

Macy could see that Adam hadn't changed much about the room. It still boasted a warm, bright yellow with large, white cabinets. The countertops were a dark brown-colored granite. Like the rest of the house, this room was inviting, and Adam only added to the atmosphere as he started a kettle of water on the stove and prepared two mugs for the tea.

"If I remember correctly, you like honey with your tea."

"Good memory."

"The last time I was at the store, I bought some to have on hand in case you were over." He looked up at Macy with a small smile, and it was at the moment that she was certain that Adam truly was a wonderful man. All those initial fights and bad blood between them had been for nothing. She was so grateful that she was finally getting to know the real Adam.

"You didn't have to do that," she said honestly. "That was very kind of you."

"It was no trouble. I figured I'd try some in my tea tonight too. It's a new year, after all. Why not try something new?" The kettle whistled, and he pulled it from the stove before it could continue screaming.

"And how are you doing? I know the holidays have been hard on you. Is there anything I can do to make you feel better?" From the moment he opened the door, Adam could see that Macy had been a bit down.

"Nope, unfortunately, there's nothing you can do other than what you're doing. Being sweet and giving me honey with my tea," she smiled softly. The only thing that could truly help ease her pain over Hadley's death was time. Macy had to just keep going on, keep marching and putting one foot in front of the other. But being surrounded by good people, like Molly and her family, and now Adam, that was also helping. For the first time, Macy realized that she'd get there. She'd see the light at the end of this long, dark tunnel of grief, but it wouldn't be immediate.

"Well if that's all it takes, then you are welcome to join me for tea any time." He brought over multiple flavors of honey for her to choose from. Each was in the bear-shaped honey bottle. "I didn't know what you liked, so I bought the three they had at the store: clover, wildflower, and thistle."

Macy laughed as she picked up each one and placed a small drop on her finger. "I actually love all three, but let's do a little taste test first." She settled on the thistle. Adam, too, did the taste test and chose the wildflower.

"This is really good," he said after stirring the honey into his tea and taking a small sip. "I think I'll make the permanent switch to honey instead of sugar. I hear it's much healthier too."

"Absolutely. Honey is a great substitute for any sweetener."

They chatted for a while and then decided on a second cup of tea. The chamomile they were drinking was decaf, so they didn't worry with another cup. And they both chose to try the clover honey this time.

"Why don't we go sit by the fire?" Adam suggested.

"It's a little sad without having Julep here to snuggle in between."

Adam laughed. "I don't think she was snuggling. I think she was guarding you from me!" He remembered how the little dog had planted herself directly between them on the couch.

Macy laughed too. Julep could be a funny little thing. "What time is Erin coming to ride Jazzy?"

"She's coming at three o'clock. Will you be joining her?"

"Yes, I should. I'm working tomorrow, but, unless an emergency pops up, I'm only scheduled until around one o'clock." Macy was officially joining Beau's practice full-time later in the month, but for now, she was still scheduled on a part-time basis.

"Well bring your riding gear and have a go at her too. I'm sure Erin would like your perspective."

"That's not a bad idea. And if Molly's free, she

might want to ride her too. I'm sure Jazzy will love it," she joked.

"She'll probably just be happy to be one of the girls," Adam said with a wink.

When Macy finished her tea, she set her mug down on the coffee table and leaned back against Adam. He wrapped his arms around her and kissed the top of her head. Between the warm glow of the fire and his big, strong arms holding safely onto her, Macy felt at peace for the first time in months. Within two minutes, she was fast asleep.

~ Chapter 22 ~

"Wow. Am I witnessing the walk of shame? I haven't seen this since college!" Erin laughed as Macy creeped in through the back door at six o'clock the next morning.

Erin was already up, showered, and making her coffee. Julep was happily eating her food which Erin had just prepared for her. Upon seeing her mom walk through the door, Julep zoomed over to say hi, then quickly retreated back to her food dish.

"If it is, it's the saddest walk of shame ever. After two cups of tea, not even alcohol, mind you, I fell asleep on the couch."

Erin roared with laughter. "That is pretty pathetic, Mace, but hopefully you had a good night's sleep."

In fact, she had. She had no recollection of how long Adam stayed with her, but when she woke up around five-thirty, she was stretched out on the couch with a blanket pulled tightly around her. Adam, having to be at the track before sunrise, had left her a note.

Hey Sleeping Beauty – I hope you slept well. I'm off to work, but I hope I see you this afternoon. Have some tea and honey with your breakfast! Love, Adam

It was such a cute note that Macy decided to take it with her. She felt like a middle-schooler doing so but didn't care.

When Erin went upstairs to change, Macy went out to the barn to feed. The two girls agreed that they'd meet up here after work and then head over to Adam's together for Erin's trial ride on Jazzy. Molly was going to meet them there.

"Good morning, momma's loves!" She cried as she opened the doors to a chorus of whinnies. She couldn't believe that only two horses could make so much noise.

"I have some exciting news for you," she told Fitz as she poured his grain. He dug right in. "I know you're a bit distracted by your breakfast, but I'm going to tell you anyway. I'm going to take some x-rays of your leg this week, and if it looks good, you're going to start going out in the dry-lot for some light turnout!"

Macy had every reason to believe Fitz was healing as he should be. He was completely sound in his stall and on their walks together. After some light turn-out and with continued hand-walks, he should be ready for full turnout within another month or so.

"I'm hoping you can be ridden again sometime this spring!"

As she set about doing her morning barn chores – letting Hunter out in the dry-lot, opening up the barn, throwing hay, mucking stalls, and filling water buckets – Macy found herself humming softly. She realized that she felt better than she had in a longtime, as if a weight had been lifted. As if the vision of her life was not quite so murky. While she didn't know the true reason for this burst of happiness, she knew that her friends and family, as well as her newfound passion with Adam, had something to do with it. *I have a long way to go before I'm back to normal, but it's a start.*

~~~~~

"Easy now, little lady, I'm not gonna hurt ya," Beau cooed to his patient later that morning. He was trying to take the temperature of a filly who was mildly
~~~~~

colicking. Macy, holding the lead, also talked softly, doing her best to soothe the horse.

"Her temp is normal," Beau announced a moment later. "And since I hear gut sounds on both sides and her heartrate is only slightly elevated, I'd say we're looking at a gas colic. I'm going to give her some banamine to help with the pain, and we'll stay here and monitor her for a bit. If she starts to get painful again, we'll do a rectal exam and tube her."

As the owner put the filly back into her stall, Beau and Macy made their way to their trucks. Beau flipped open his metal clipboard and began taking some notes while Macy organized some supplies in the back.

"Oh guess who I just heard from? Your dear friend Cassidy!" Macy said with a wicked grin. While everything had worked out for the best with Beau and Molly after Cassidy had played her little trick, hearing Cassidy's name only conjured up bad memories for Beau. Macy knew this, of course, but sometimes she couldn't resist having a little fun.

"Mace, anyone ever tell you that you're a bit on the rotten side?" Beau said with an equally wicked grin.

"Ha – yes, I've heard that before. You know I can't be serious all the time!"

"I'll never admit to sayin this, but I do appreciate your humor at times." He was secretly happy to see some of the spark returning to Macy's eyes. She almost seemed herself today. "What did *our dear friend* Cassidy have to say for herself?"

"She texted earlier letting me know she got the interview at New Bolton. She asked if she could stay with me when she comes in for it. She doesn't have a date scheduled yet."

"New Bolton, huh? Well, best of luck to her. Now don't be upset when I don't drop by to say hey while she's here." He winked at her.

"What? I was going to have you and Molly over for a big, fancy dinner so we could all visit together. Shame. I guess I'll cancel it." She started laughing to herself.

"You just crack yourself up, don't ya?" Beau couldn't wait to tell Molly how the normal, spirited Macy had returned. He hoped she was here to stay.

Macy was laughing so hard she had tears in her eyes. "Oh Beau, I'm so sorry," she sputtered. "You're just such a good sport that I can't help but tease you."

"You do know that I'm your boss, and I have the right to fire you at any time." Beau said, starting to laugh as well.

"No!" Macy shouted as she clutched her stomach which was starting to hurt. "Don't fire me – I'll be good, I promise!" When Beau looked doubtful, she added, "Pinky swear, Beau!"

At that, he completely lost it and both doubled over with laughter. It felt so good to see the old, silly Macy again. And it felt good to *be* the old, silly Macy again. She couldn't remember the last time she laughed that hard.

"Alright my rotten employee," Beau said as he whipped some tears from laughter from his eyes, "let's go check on our little lady again."

~~~~~

"It's my favorite three amigos!" Adam declared as Erin, Macy, and Molly walked through his barn. Macy had always loved this barn at the old Radnor place. It was actually a shedrow, but it was shaped in an L, so it had a very English flair to it. In the center of the L, the Radnor's had planted some shrubbery and placed a few
~~~~~

benches, and Macy was pleased to see that Adam had left things as they were.

"She's this way," Adam said as he led the girls down the long side of the row. Jazzy was stabled in the last stall in the corner. "Would you like to get her ready, or do you want to watch me do it?"

"I'll do it," Erin said. "I want to get the whole Jazzy experience," she smiled. This was always a good idea when getting a new horse – be as hands-on as possible. Tack up, pick hooves, brush them, you name it – it was always good for the potential new owner to get to know the horse as well as possible before bringing him or her home.

Erin brought Jazzy out of her stall and placed her into cross-ties. The mare stood quietly, which was a good sign considering she had been at Adam's place for less than twenty-four hours. Adam brought out her brush caddy, and Erin and Molly went to work removing her winter blanket and brushing her out. Macy hung back with Adam to watch.

Erin picked out each of Jazzy's hooves and complimented the mare on her good manners. While she didn't seem to be loving all the attention, Jazzy didn't particularly mind it either. She was a horse who knew her job, and her job was to do what the humans asked of her.

"I brought my saddle with me, I hope you don't mind," Erin said to Adam. "I wanted to see how it fit her. It's a Devoucoux, and I've had it for years – I'd love to make it work with her."

Adam brought over a saddle pad and when Erin placed the saddle on top, it was practically a perfect fit. "She's shaped very much like Ruby, my old mare, so I was crossing my fingers it would fit."

"Looks pretty perfect to me," said Molly who was helping to adjust it. "Hopefully Jazzy likes it!"

After Jazzy was tacked and ready to go, Adam led them to the sand ring that flanked the left side of the barn. The ring was a newer addition, built not too long before Mrs. Radnor sold the farm to Adam. She was older and past her riding prime, but she had the ring built so her granddaughter could work her show ponies over fences in a confined space.

"I can lunge her first if you'd like, but she's not one that typically needs it. She will usually get right down to work. You're a new rider though, so I wouldn't be surprised if she tries to test you a bit."

"Let's see how she is without lunging." Erin hand-walked her around the perimeter of the ring, allowing Jazzy to look at her new surroundings. She took it all in with wide-eyed interest, but still obeyed Erin's commands. After one circuit, Erin brought her to the mounting block.

"I can see her smiling from here," Molly said to Macy. "With everything she's been through with Kevin over the last year, I think she really needs this."

"Yes, a very welcomed distraction."

As soon as Erin mounted, she checked the girth and settled herself deeper in the saddle. When she asked Jazzy to move off at the walk, Jazzy refused. She just stood there.

"Here we go," Adam called. "The test begins!"

Erin laughed as she urged Jazzy on again. Jazzy, her ears flat back and nose crinkled in unhappiness, continued to stand stock still.

Again Erin squeezed her forward, kicking Jazzy in the sides a bit harder. Still no movement from the horse. Erin repeated her request, this time sinking her spurs into the horse's sides. Nothing.

"Okay, little lady," Erin said. "You asked for it. GET UP!" With that shout, Erin flipped her crop forward so she held it like a baton, whipped it back, and cracked Jazzy hard on the rear-end. The horse leaped forward and took off into a startled trot. The three could hear Erin praising Jazzy for finally moving forward, and they saw her bring her back into a nice, controlled walk.

The rest of the ride went off without incident. Jazzy had tested Erin, and the confident rider had clearly passed. Erin put her through her paces in each direction, falling in love with her floaty trot and smooth-as-silk canter.

Molly hopped on the horse after Erin had finished and returned ten minutes later grinning from ear-to-ear.

"You've got something with this one," she said to her sister. "If you don't want her, I'll take her!"

Macy hadn't dressed to ride. An emergency had come up at work, so she had met Erin and Molly at Adam's. She would have loved to have ridden the mare, but she had a feeling there'd be other opportunities.

"I'd like to have her vetted, but if she passes, I'll take her," Erin said as she extended her hand to Adam. The two were beaming as they shook on it. Then Erin turned to Macy. "Would you like to do the pre-purchase exam, or should I ask Beau?"

Macy laughed. "Of course I'll do it. Let me know what time works tomorrow, and I'll get you on the books!"

"I hope I get the family discount," Erin joked with Molly. "I hear that Doctor Bridges is expensive!"

"He is not!" Molly cried. "And I think we can work something out," she winked. "But here's another question. Is Jazzy going home to mom and dad's or will she go to Mace's?"

"I have given that some thought, and I was thinking, if it's okay with you, Mace, I'd like to bring Jazzy to your place. Since I'm staying there, it would be nice to walk outside and see her. How do you think the boys would feel about a girl moving in?"

"Are you kidding? They'd love it!"

"What about you? You've already been so kind to open up your house to me. You don't have to open your barn as well…even though I'd love it!"

"Erin, you are family. There's always room for family. And besides, it will be nice to have someone to ride with." The two girls embraced.

"Well since she'll be going so close, if she vets out, you can just ride her next door!" Adam said.

~ Chapter 23 ~

Macy and Erin were amazed at how quickly Jazzy settled in at her new home. Having passed her pre-purchase exam earlier that afternoon, Erin tacked her up and prepared to ride next door to Macy's. Adam thought that Jazzy would be fine hacking out alone, but just to play it safe, he tacked Pitcher and rode alongside the young mare. While the two were heading over, Macy drove back to her farm to make sure Jazzy's stall would be ready for her arrival.

They had decided to put her in the first stall on the left as you walked into the barn. This way she'd be directly across from the boys. They would all be able to see and smell each other, but they wouldn't be able to touch. Having been a racehorse, Jazzy was used to other horses being nearby, but she hadn't been turned out with any, especially a gelding, since she was a yearling. It would take some time for her, and the boys, to adjust to each other.

Jazzy hacked over to her new stable like an old pro. Adam stayed around for a bit and chatted with the girls while they gave everyone some hay to snack on.

"She just walked right into her stall like she owned the place," Macy commented, happy to see the horse settling in well.

"You have to remember," Adam said, sitting astride Pitcher just outside of the barn's entrance. "All racehorses are very well-traveled. They're used to being shipped from track to track. They learn quickly that their stalls are their safe havens and most relax pretty quickly, even in new settings."

Hunter and Fitz were very interested in their new roommate. Each stuck their heads into the barn aisle and flipped their upper lips, trying to get a better smell of Jazzy.

"Weirdos," Erin said with a laugh as she watched the boys. "Adam, how do you recommend getting them used to each other?"

Adam looked at Macy. "Has Hunter been turned out with mares before?"

"He has. He couldn't care in the slightest who his pasture mate is as long as they don't get in the way of his food! Fitz, on the other hand, is in the same boat as Jazzy. He was in training until he was injured. I took him not long after, so he hasn't been turned out with anyone – mare or gelding. I'm going to start him on limited turnout by himself soon."

"Okay, sounds like Hunter will be the middle man. He'll get to know Jazzy first, and then the three can go together eventually. I'd start though by riding out with Macy on Hunter – let the two get to know each other during a ride where they can't get too close. Do that a few times, then they can go into a small paddock together. Give them plenty of hay too. Hopefully Hunter will be more concerned about the hay than the new girl."

"That's very possible," laughed Macy. "Hunter doesn't like missing any meals!"

While Erin busied herself caring for Jazzy and organizing her feed and tack, (most was still over at her mom's – she'd have to make a few trips to move it all), Adam and Macy talked for a few more moments.

"Do you have time to go for a ride with me? Weather's beautiful today."

He was right. For January third, it was a picture-perfect day: sunny, clear, no wind, and about forty-five degrees.

"Sure," she replied. "Just give me a minute to get Hunter ready." She bounded into the barn, brushed

Hunter down, picked his hooves, and then tacked up as quickly as she could. Adam was right; it was a gorgeous day to ride.

Erin waved them off as they headed straight to the back of Macy's property, walking in between two fenced-in pastures. It had been about a week since Macy had ridden last, and it felt good to be back in the saddle. Hunter, also happy to be out, had an extra spring in his step.

"So I don't think I ever asked you – how was Middleburg?" The two were enjoying an easy stroll with the horses walking side by side.

"It was great," Adam said with a smile. "It was nice catching up with old friends and neighbors. I haven't been away long, but I almost forgot what a nice area it is – truly devoted to the horse in every way. The only thing missing…was you." He reached over, placed his finger under Macy's chin, and turned it toward him. With a shy smile he leaned over and kissed her gently.

Macy, warmed by his touched, blushed ever so slightly. "It's been quite some time since I visited. Maybe we could plan a trip…at some point." She still wasn't sure if she was ready to take their relationship, whatever it was right now, to the next level by traveling together. Erin had asked her recently if Adam was officially her boyfriend yet, but Macy didn't know. Truth was, she still wasn't ready for any type of commitment. She was still trying to find her stride in life again. And while Macy still beat herself up for complicating life by adding Adam into the mix, she also reasoned that someone who made her feel so good couldn't be that bad for her. *I guess time will tell.*

"I'm ready whenever you are. I'll be heading out with Etch on his road to the Derby, hopefully, that is, but when I'm home, I'm always up for an adventure with the pretty girl next door."

When they came to a clearing where Macy always let Hunter run, he started to jig a bit. "Mind if we have a little gallop? Hunter's ready to go!"

"Mace, I'll gallop with you to the ends of the earth," Adam said seriously.

Unsure of how to respond to that, Macy just gave Hunter his head and soon they were flying across the ground. Even with a few seconds head start, Pitcher, all thoroughbred, drew alongside and matched them stride for stride. After a few strides like that, Pitcher began to draw away, but Adam, wanting to stay with Macy, pulled him back a bit.

They both pulled up at the edge of the field where the woods began. Macy, cheeks bright red and eyes dancing, laughed as she gave Hunter a good pat.

"He's no thoroughbred, but the boy does love a good run! You didn't have to hold Pitcher back. Hunter knows where he stands among the horse world. He lived in Kentucky for years; he's been beat many a times by ex-racehorses." Hunter, a warmblood, was not bred for racing. While he moved beautifully, especially in the dressage ring, he simply could not compete with a long and leggy thoroughbred who moved flawlessly yet swiftly with minimal effort.

"Pitcher just wanted to keep things competitive," he said with a smile.

They turned their horses for a leisurely walk back. The sun was beginning to set, but they'd still make it back before dark.

"Thanks for letting Erin look at your retirees first. I know she really appreciated having her pick. All three were gorgeous though. Did you find homes for Sampson and Lighter yet?"

"I think so. Cindy, one of my exercise riders, has

a friend looking for a hunter prospect. I think she does some low level dressage too, and she's interested in Sampson. Her friend looked at him the other day at Pimlico but hasn't stopped by the farm to ride him yet. Lighter is leaving tomorrow – going to Aaron Wilson's farm. She's going to be a polo pony."

"I thought you said Lighter was kind of timid."

"She is, but she's also coming four, so she's young and trainable. And if anyone can turn an OTTB into a dynamite polo pony, it's Aaron. He and his family take great care of their horses, so I'm happy he wants her."

"Perfect. I love happy endings. What do you do with the retirees that are harder to place? Maybe one that's been injured and is either a light-riding or companion-only horse?"

"Those are definitely harder to find homes for, as you know. But since I've always had my own home farm, if you will, I just hang onto them until I can place them. I had one for almost a year before I found him a home as a companion to a retired foxhunter. It's not huge, of course, but there is still a need for those types of horses too. Those homes just don't come along as often."

Macy felt her heart overflow. Many trainers helped place their retirees, but few would hold onto one for almost a year until the right home came along. Macy had truly misjudged Adam; he absolutely was one of the good guys, and she was ashamed it had taken her so long to see it.

As they approached the barn, Adam veered to the right, heading back to his place, but not before he leaned over and gave Macy one last kiss.

After putting Hunter up and feeding him and Fitz, Macy jogged back to the house, a spring in her step despite the cold. She was in her bedroom changing out of her riding clothes when her phone rang. She was excited to see that it was Cassidy.

"Cass!" Macy was excited to hear from her friend. They texted regularly, but there was nothing like a good old gab-fest on the phone.

"Someone sounds happy! How are things working out with our favorite neighbor and racehorse trainer, Adam Cleary?"

Macy filled Cassidy in on some of the details. "We just got back from a great ride, so that's why I'm so happy."

Cassidy wasn't fooled. "Hmm, sure it is."

"Okay, okay, the ride *and* the company were pretty good."

"That sounds more like it," she laughed. "So New Bolton called. They scheduled my interview for the twentieth. Can I come stay with you for a bit? I'm going to take the whole week off. I figured I'd visit with you for a bit, and then be on hand for New Bolton. If all goes well, it will be more than a one day thing."

"Absolutely, come whenever and stay until whenever. Erin and I always have room at our bachelorette pad."

"Perfect – thank you! I figured I'd fly in on the eighteenth or nineteenth and then leave around the twenty-fourth or so. I'll let you know when I have everything finalized. And no need to worry about picking me up at the airport; I'll rent a car. Or, on second thought, maybe I'll drive instead of fly." She paused to consider this. "Either way, I'll keep you posted."

"Sounds great – can't wait to see you!"

~ Chapter 24 ~

The first month of the New Year passed by in a blur. Beau hired Macy on full-time, and between her work calls, her horses, and Adam, she hardly had a free moment to herself. But she liked being busy; it kept her mind off other things, like the fact that she still felt like a zombie, as if she was moving through the shadows of someone else's life even though she knew it was her own.

Macy and Erin had settled into a nice routine. They took turns doing morning feedings with Macy almost always home before Erin for evenings. Erin was taking things slow with Jazzy, and she and Macy hacked out often, weather permitting, for nice, easy rides through the countryside. Erin wanted Jazzy to have some downtime to realize she wasn't a racehorse anymore. If all went well, she was hoping to start her into a training program sometime in the spring or early summer.

Jazzy and Hunter had been turned out together, and things went smoothly. The ever-dependable Hunter could not have cared less that he was sharing his pasture with a cute, young mare. He was only after one thing – his hay!

Fitz was now on light turnout with Hunter, (when Hunter wasn't babysitting Jazzy), and progressing just as he should be. His injury had required lots of downtime and stall rest, but now, almost six months later, he was close to being good as new. As long as he didn't have any setbacks, Macy would start lightly riding him sometime during the spring.

And as far as Adam, well, the two had agreed not to label whatever their relationship was. Erin called him *Macy's boyfriend*, Molly called them *friends with benefits*. For right now, Macy just called him *her neighbor*. She still couldn't think beyond about the future and just tried to take each day as it came, one at a time. Adam understood this and didn't push or pressure Macy for anything, for which she was grateful.

But even though they weren't officially an item, it didn't stop Macy from fantasizing about him all day long and looking forward to seeing him at the end of the day. Adam spent all day at the track, gearing up for the upcoming racing season with Etch. He would be making his first start of the year in the Sam F. Davis Stakes. Everyone had high hopes for the three year old – he was definitely the horse to watch.

After returning home from work, Macy parked her truck and entered the house through the sunroom that also served as a mudroom. She was immediately greeted by the scent of Erin's cooking; a warm meal was brewing in the crockpot.

"Hi," Erin said as she laid out some dinner plates. "How was work? I'm making chicken n' dumplings for dinner."

"Well aren't we just an old married couple," Macy laughed. She had to admit, she was so happy that Erin had moved in. Of course, it hurt watching her friend struggle through a divorce, but Macy was happy to have some company.

"We really are. I had an appointment up this way around three o'clock, so I just called it a day after that. I fed the horses, Julep, and, of course, I started dinner in the crock before work this morning."

"You are wonder woman!"

"Right? Everyone thinks that except for Kevin. Oh well, his loss."

"His loss is my gain!"

Erin laughed at that. "We really are a mess. And it sounds like our brood is expanding. When does Cassidy arrive?"

"Tomorrow, probably late afternoon. Which reminds me, I need to make up the guest room." Cassidy had decided to drive to Maryland and would be staying in the room that Hadley had used to store her exercise equipment. There was a day bed in there that would work just fine for petite Cassidy. No one had touched Hadley's old bedroom though. Macy just couldn't bear to move in there even though she knew that it was unhealthy to leave everything as it was. Moving in and redecorating just seemed too arduous a task at the moment. All in good time.

The girls dug into their dinner, each quiet for a moment as the warm dumplings filled their hungry stomachs.

"These dumplings are excellent. Nice and fluffy."

"Thanks," Erin said. "We Sorrenson girls have perfected them over the years. This is Molly's favorite meal, so this is a dish we've prepared many, many times."

"Speaking of Molly, how has she been? I haven't talked to her in about a week."

"She's fine," answered Erin. "I honestly think she and my mom were a little miffed at first that I had decided to keep Jazzy here. They understood, of course, that it was just more convenient to have her right outside, but still. I think they wanted us all to be together."

"I can understand that. I think Molly wanted you two to train together, but it's not like you guys can't. We're literally five minutes down the road. And I have a youngster too now, which is crazy to think about. I'm, selfishly, glad you're here. It will be nice to have an extra set of eyes watching as I bring Fitz along. Not only for training purposes, but for safety too."

"Exactly. See? I'm helping out a friend in need.

I'm keeping you safe!" Erin laughed to herself, partly because she was being silly, but also because that's exactly what she had said to her mom and Molly, that it would be unwise to leave Macy all alone.

Erin cleared her throat and continued. "So I have some news. Kevin officially served me with divorce papers today."

"What? I can't believe it. I thought you guys were going to continue with counseling for a bit?"

"I thought so too, but I guess he had other plans. But you know what? It's okay. Our issue wasn't one that could really be resolved anyway. There's no real compromise – it's not like you can have half a baby, you know?" Erin said sarcastically.

"You're handling it remarkably well."

"I'll probably have a nice, long cry in the shower later," she said with a smirk. "To tell you the truth, he beat me to it. I met with my attorney yesterday and had the papers drawn up myself. It's time. We've reached the end of our road together, so to speak."

Macy reached out and took Erin's hand. "For what it's worth, I was really pulling for you guys, but honestly, I think you're making the right decision. You need to think about yourself first and foremost, and that's exactly what you're doing. It's *your* life, not his."

"Which is why I got Jazzy! Screw Kevin and his wanting a baby. Screw him and his need for a family. I have my own family! So what if they have four legs?" Erin smiled at Macy to let her know that she was just being facetious, but still, she was right. A family didn't necessarily have to include two-legged children. A family could be anything; it just needed one main ingredient: love.

"You're absolutely right, and I'm proud of you. Forget him!"

"I'm going to dress Jazzy up as a baby, put a bonnet on her head, and a rattle in her teeth and send him a picture. I'll be like, I got my baby – good luck finding yours!" Erin was clearly on a roll, and she had Macy laughing hysterically.

"I'm joking, of course, and I most likely will have a good cry tonight, but I am in a good place with it. It's not like this is breaking news; we've been riding this rollercoaster for much longer than I let on. And I do wish him the best. I wish I could have been enough for him even without a family, but it's okay that I wasn't. I'm enough for me."

Macy agreed wholeheartedly. She, too, needed to learn how to be enough for herself.

~~~~~

Later that evening, Macy went upstairs to make up the guest room for Cassidy. She put fresh sheets on the bed, placed some towels and washcloths on the nightstand, and gave the room a quick dusting. Then she took a picture on snapchat and added the text: *Room is ready for one Cassidy Winters!* She sent the snap off to Cass, excited that her friend would be arriving the next day.

Macy decided that her room could use a dusting as well, so she hummed softly to herself while she worked. She was so impressed with Erin's behavior. Here she was going through one of the most difficult times in her life, and she was cracking jokes about dressing up her horse and sticking it to her ex. Of course, she knew Erin was hurting inside and putting on a brave front was her way of coping, but there was a new light in her friend's eyes too. Over the past few weeks, she had seen a new foundation being built within Erin, and Macy had to
~~~~~

admit, she was jealous. *Why can't I get my head straight?*

She knew that everyone coped with grief differently, but Macy felt that she still spent more days than not walking around in a fog. It wasn't affecting her work or her daily life, at least not severely, but she realized that she spent a lot of time in the past, and she knew why.

Just the other day she and Tommy had talked about their mutual fear of forgetting their mother. As time marched on, it would be harder to recall the look on her face after she'd had an exhilarating ride, the brightness in her eyes as she welcomed Macy home for a visit from Kentucky. Their memories would fade, and that scared them to death.

"I'm going to start writing them down," Tommy had said. "And when my children are old enough and ask about their grandmother, I'm going to give them a journal full of my thoughts and memories."

It was a great idea, and Macy intended to do the same. Maybe writing the past down, bringing it front and center to the present, would help her move on a bit. Maybe it would help her to live in today again, leaving yesterday behind.

At that moment, she heard the shower turn on in Erin's guest bathroom. She hoped that her friend was having that good cry she spoke of at dinner. *Let go of your grief*, Macy thought. *Let it pour down the drain.*

~~~~~

"Welcome to Maryland!" Macy squealed as she opened the door and wrapped Cassidy into a big hug.

Cassidy, petite, green-eyed, and redheaded, happily embraced Macy, dropping her luggage on the porch with a thud as she did so. She had driven straight
~~~~~

through from Lexington, rising early to get a jumpstart on the day.

"Come on in. It's freezing outside," Macy said, ushering her friend into the warm house. Macy had gotten off work a bit early, so she started a fire in the kitchen fireplace, and had a stew cooking in the crockpot.

"Wow, Mace," Cass said in awe as she looked around. "Your place is gorgeous. What a cozy home you've made for yourself."

"Well, I can't take all the credit. This was our family home that my mom designed and decorated. I've just never left." She laughed as she took Cassidy's coat and hung it in the entryway closet. "Come, let me show you around." At that moment, she heard barking at the back of the house. "Oh wait, I forgot to let Julep in."

Macy hurried to the back door where an impatient Julep was waiting. She had heard Cassidy's arrival and was anxious to meet the new guest.

"Cass, this is Mint Julep – she's my resident mouser. Julep, this is Cass. We used to work together in Kentucky." The two girls laughed at the formal introduction and as Julep jumped straight into Cassidy's arms. "Julep is very shy. Hates new people. Not friendly in the slightest." Macy smiled as her love-bug of a dog was anything but shy.

"So, give me the grand tour. And I want to see the horse kids too!" It had been months since Cassidy had seen Fitz, whom she had helped care for in the hospital, so she had been looking forward to seeing the handsome dappled grey, as well as Hunter.

Macy showed Cassidy the main level, including the large kitchen and cozy study. Then she led her upstairs and showed her the guest room. "These are your accommodations, Lady Cassidy," Macy said with a fake British accent. "I hope you will find them satisfactory."

Cassidy laughed. "Someone's been watching too much Downton Abbey."

"Yes, I admit it. At night when I get in bed, I watch an episode before I fall asleep. Why couldn't I have been born a Crawley?"

"Well this isn't Downton, but I'd say you have a pretty nice life here."

"Agreed. And I'm so happy you're here. I have dinner in the crock, and Erin will be home soon."

Quickly Macy gave Cassidy a brief update on Erin's divorce, as well as mentioned her new horse.

"I'm heartbroken that she's going through all this," said Macy, "but she's been a wonderful roommate. I didn't realize how lonely I was."

"I'm happy she's here for you too. And I love that she got a new horse. New Year, new horse – new life. I love fresh starts." Cassidy was thinking to herself that she was grateful that Macy had allowed them to have a fresh start as co-workers and then as friends. She was still beyond embarrassed over her behavior with Beau and Molly, but she was thankful it didn't cause any lasting damage. And it served as a wake-up call; she needed to get herself together or she wasn't going to have a single friend. When she mentioned all of this to Macy, not long after Beau officially moved to Maryland, Macy hadn't hesitated to give her a second chance – and Cassidy wasn't going to blow it.

The girls put their coats on and went outside into the chilly air to see the horses. It was time to feed dinner anyway. Julep loped alongside the girls, happy to have a visitor, and happy to be back in the barn chasing mice.

"Wow, Mace, Fitz looks great!" Cassidy went in his stall while he was busy at his feed bucket and inspected his legs. "Looks like you'll be on his back in no time."

"I hope so. And this is Jazzy, Erin's new mare." The mare pinned her ears as the two girls entered the stall, but she didn't move as they reached out to stoke her silky neck.

"Oh you're an opinionated one, aren't you?" Cassidy laughed at the mare's behavior.

"That she is," said Macy. "But her bark is worse than her bite. She wouldn't hurt a fly, but she's all mare."

"I love a good spunky mare. And speaking of, how's Gypsy?" Like everyone else in the hospital, Cassidy had loved caring for Gypsy, Molly's filly.

"She's perfect, just as you'd expect. She and Molly are a match made in heaven." Macy smiled as she thought about her best friend and her beautiful horse.

"I'm so happy to hear it. And there's another fan-favorite – Hunter!" She skipped over to the big chestnut who had just finished his grain and stuck his head out over the stall door. Cassidy wrapped her arms around his strong neck and gave him a hug. "I've missed you boy."

Cassidy scratched behind Hunter's ears and kissed him on the nose as Macy threw multiple large flakes of hay into each stall. Then Cassidy filled water buckets and checked to make sure all doors and gates were shut and locked. After they finished, they turned out the barn lights and walked back up to the house, Julep lagging behind, wishing she were still hunting rodents.

Erin was just walking through the front door as the other two entered the kitchen. Julep went racing to greet Erin, and Erin scooped the dog into her arms and carried her into the kitchen.

"Erin, this is Cassidy Winters. Cass, this is my roommate Erin."

The two girls shook hands and exchanged pleasantries. Erin knew the part Cassidy had played in Molly and Beau's brief break up, but Macy had assured her that Cassidy had learned her lesson and had changed for the better.

"I'm going to run upstairs and change, and then I'll be back down to set the table for dinner," said Erin as she turned to walk out the door.

The girls busied themselves putting the finishing touches on dinner and Cassidy was smiling as she opened a bottle of wine and poured it into glasses Macy had placed on the counter. "Okay, I'm moving in. This is a total bachelorette pad. Beautiful house. Two fun girls. A cute dog, and horses right outside."

"And don't forget the hunky neighbor next door," Erin said with a wink, walking back into the room wearing jeans and a sweater.

"Oh that's right!" Cassidy said, turning around to grin at Macy. "A love interest makes this place even better. What's the status with you two now?"

Macy blushed the tiniest shade of red. She hated being the center of attention in situations like this. Situations where she didn't know the answer. "Honestly, I'm not completely sure. We agreed not to talk about it for right now and not label ourselves. I think he'd be fine with getting a bit more serious, but he knows I'm not ready. So we're just kind of going with the flow."

"Good for you guys." Erin said with an easy smile, grabbing bowls and silverware to set the table.

"I know. The truth is that some days I kick myself for starting anything with him in the first place. My life is pretty complicated at this point, and I don't need to add to it. But," Macy paused and blushed again, "he's kind of irresistible."

"Now I really want to meet him!" Cassidy laughed. "And does he have a brother?"

The three girls gathered around the dinner table to enjoy their bowls of hearty beef stew, salad, and a fresh

French baguette. They chatted easily about anything and everything, Cassidy filling them in on her interview the next day. After they finished their meals, they took their wine glasses and headed into the family room to lounge in front of the fireplace. Julep nestled in the blankets on the couch curled up tightly against Macy.

~ Chapter 25 ~

"So she got the job? Good for her!" Adam said one week later after Macy told him Cassidy had accepted a position at New Bolton Center.

"I know, I'm so excited for her. She starts sometime in May, so that gives her a bit of time to figure everything out with the move. I told her she could stay with me and Erin, but she's thinking she should find a place closer to the hospital. We're about an hour south."

"That makes sense. If she gets called in for an emergency, she can't be an hour away."

Macy sat on Adam's bed watching him pack. Etch was running in his first Derby prep race, the Sam F. Davis Stakes at Tampa Bay Downs in Florida. She was surprised to realize that she was going to miss him in the five days he'd be away. Things had grown so easy between them. Of course, there were days when they argued about the smallest things, but Macy had to admit that she and Adam were good together. They complemented each other, understood the other's work, and had many common interests. Molly and Erin both told her that she should "lock him down," but she wasn't quite ready for that. She knew they'd take the next step at some point, but it wouldn't be Macy's doing.

Almost as if reading her mind, Adam looked up at her, his strong jawline taunt, his expression serious. "I'm going to miss you, you know."

Macy melted. "I'm going to miss you too."

"Really? Have I finally melted the Ice Queen's heart?" They laughed. He had taken to calling her the Ice Queen recently, and while it hurt her that he perceived her to be cold, she hadn't exactly given him the warm and fuzzies. Overall, she found it funny.

"No, I'm still the cold-hearted bitch you think I am," she said with a wink. "I am going to miss you though, but don't let that go to your head."

"Don't you worry. I don't take anything for granted with you. I was wondering though," he paused to clear his throat. "What do you say we head out of town for a little getaway, maybe next week when I get back?"

"Umm, next week also happens to be Valentine's Day, so maybe I should take a pass."

"What if I promise not to give you flowers or buy you any jewelry?" He said, reaching out to caress her cheek with his thumb.

"I suppose that might work. I'm not much of a jewelry person anyway," she said, closing her eyes and leaning into his hand.

"Then it's done. I'll plan something and surprise you. No flowers, no jewelry, no chocolates."

"Hey, I never said anything about chocolate. Chocolate is *always* acceptable."

Adam smiled softly. "I wish I weren't going away. I won't be able to stop thinking about you."

"I've been told I'm hard to forget."

And with that, Adam reached under her sweater and skillfully unsnapped her bra strap. "What do you say you give me a little something to remember you by?"

~~~~~

Macy was at a call when Etch was running, so she wasn't able to watch the horse's impressive win in the grade three stakes race. She could hear the bliss in Adam's voice when he called her later to tell her the good news.

"He did it, baby, he did it!" Adam shouted. Macy could imagine him pumping his fist in the air, triumphant
~~~~~

in his horse's victory.

They talked about the specifics of the race for a few minutes, and then Adam had to go. Before he signed off he mentioned their getaway. "So I made reservations for next Thursday through Sunday. Do you think you'll be able to get off?"

"Yep. I already talked to Beau and told him I'd like a few days off, and he was fine with it. I just need to let him know it's a definite."

"Perfect, I can't wait to whisk you away and have you all to myself."

"Where are we going?"

"Maybe I'm not allowed to give you any gifts for the holiday, but I can at least keep this a surprise."

~~~~~

"So he didn't give you a single hint?" Asked Molly the following afternoon. It had been a mild day, so after her ride on Gypsy, she drove over to spend the afternoon with Macy and her sister. With the sun shining through the large windows of the sunroom, they were warm and cozy.

"He said we're going for three nights, and that we're not traveling too far. No need to bring a passport. Those were his exact words. I'm glad about that though because I think my passport has expired. It didn't get used too often as I drove back and forth to Kentucky over the last ten years," Macy laughed.

"Well it's very romantic, this secret little rendezvous," said Molly.

"Yes, it is about time he stepped up his game," grinned Erin, "you know, if he wants to make you more than just his lady lover."

"But I don't want him to make me more than that.
~~~~~

I'm fine with having a discreet affair!"

"And there's nothing wrong with a little affair here and there, as long as no one's married, that is." Erin had been thinking herself that it was high time she went out and had a little fun of her own.

Thankfully for Macy, the talk soon turned to horses. Erin had been taking Jazzy out almost every day, and the mare seemed to enjoy her romps through the woods, encountering new obstacles in stride.

"She is such a wench on the ground, pinning her ears all the time, but she's my wench. And she is wonderful under saddle; you can tell she's one of those horses who just likes to get out and work. Adam was absolutely right about her."

"There's nothing quite like a Thoroughbred," agreed Molly. The two girls had grown up riding ex-racers almost exclusively, so they were very familiar with the highly-athletic, yet sensitive breed.

"I'm not going to lie, I'm a little nervous about bringing Fitz around. He'll be my first Thoroughbred in years. Mom's foxhunter, Crimson, was probably the last one I rode regularly. She was a doll, of course, but that was probably right around the time I got Hunter – ages ago!"

"You'll be fine," insisted Erin. "You're an excellent rider, so you won't have any issues. But if you do, Moll and I are here to help."

Macy wondered if the Sorrenson girls knew how much she had come to depend on them. They had become more than friends; they were truly family, and she couldn't imagine a day without one of them. Being able to come home to Erin every night was a godsend. Just that extra presence in the house, knowing that she was down the hall at night, comforted Macy.

"Back to your romantic vacay," Erin said,

breaking Macy out of her reverie, “did he mention anything about fancy dinners or whatnot? Should you bring a nicer dress?”

“That’s a good question. He never said. I’ll send him a text while I’m thinking about it.”

Macy typed off a quick note and sent it on its way. A moment later, she had her answer.

Yes, we are going to two nice dinners. Also bring your riding clothes.

Macy read the message aloud to the girls, and Molly squealed. “Oh a riding vacation! How lovely!”

Even though Macy had some trepidation about the impending trip alone with Adam, she had to admit that she was starting to look forward to the little getaway.

Later that evening after Molly left and Erin had retired to her room for the night, Macy pulled out a suitcase and started packing for the trip. She knew they were staying relatively close, so she packed warm-weather clothing, her breeches, her favorite Ariat vest, and her trusty pair of field boots. *Now, what to do about the dresses.*

As Macy roamed through her closet, she realized that most of her dresses were summery, and they wouldn’t do for a fancy dinner in February. She decided that paired with a simple white cardigan and a flashy silk scarf, her favorite little black dress would work just fine. But unless she could borrow something from Erin or Molly, Macy would have to make a trip to the store tomorrow. Like Molly, Macy considered shopping mostly a chore, so she crossed her fingers that her friends could come to the rescue.

She then made her way over to the drawer that housed her underwear and bras and pulled out the little lingerie she owned. *Should I bring this?* She'd told him over and over that she didn't want a relationship and wasn't looking for love, (hence the "Ice Queen" nickname). So if she showed up rocking the little bit of Victoria's Secret that she owned, would she be sending mixed messages? *What would the girls do?* Molly would probably play it safe and leave it home, but Erin would definitely bring it. Figuring she could decide in the heat of the moment, Macy threw the lingerie in the bag, burying it so it wasn't visible the moment she opened the bag.

She texted the girls:

Macy: Do either of you have a wintery dress I could borrow for the trip?
Erin: Why are you texting me? Walk down the hall and knock on my door!
Macy: I didn't want to bother you in case you were sleeping.
Erin: It's only 9!
Macy: Some people go to bed early.
Erin: Walk down the hall!
Macy: Okay I'm coming!
Molly: Lol you two! Let me know if none of Erin's work. I probably have something.
Macy: Thanks loves!

~ Chapter 26 ~

Adam pulled up in front of Macy's in his black Land Rover and knocked on the front door. He looked like he had stepped out of the pages of *Town & Country Magazine* because he was sporting well-cut jeans, a blue plaid shirt, and his usual Barbour jacket. When Macy answered, Julep came careening around the corner and jumped into Adam's arms.

"Looks like someone's excited to see you," Macy said with a smile.

"What can I say? All the ladies love me." Adam scratched the little pup behind her ears as he leaned over to give Macy a quick kiss. "Are you ready to go?"

"Yes, all set. That suitcase needs to go, as well as my boot and helmet bags." Macy ended up finding a simple wool dress of Erin's that fit perfectly. It was hunter green, and she had decided to pair it with her tan knee boots and the same white cardigan.

As Adam loaded her luggage in his SUV, Macy gave Julep a hug and kiss goodbye. She was going to miss her fur-babies, but she knew they'd all be in good hands with Erin who was on horse and doggy-sitting duty.

"I think I've mentioned this before," Macy said as soon as they started down the road, "but it bears repeating. I hate surprises. Can you tell me where we're going?"

Adam laughed. "Okay fine. We're going to Middleburg. I wanted to show you around town for New Year's, but since you couldn't make it then, I decided another trip was in order. We're staying at the Salamander Resort."

"We are? I've never been there but have seen

pictures. It looks gorgeous!" Macy had recently read a review about the luxury equestrian resort and spa in one of her favorite publications, *Horse & Style Magazine*. "I'm assuming we're going to ride while we're there?" Why else would he have asked her to bring her gear?

"We're riding while we're away, but I'm not telling you more than that. I want to keep a few things secret!" He smiled at Macy as he reached out to hold her hand.

They made great time and arrived in Middleburg just over two hours later. As Adam handed the car keys to the valet and grabbed their bags, Macy made her way into the resort. She stood speechless in the entryway – Salamander was breathtaking. The lobby was exquisite, not overly ostentatious, but pristine and neat. And, best of all, there were equestrian touches everywhere, from floor to ceiling, the décor was one massive nod to all things horses.

"This place is unreal," Macy said as Adam came up behind her. "Send Julep because I'm never leaving."

Adam laughed as he headed to the check-in counter, "I knew you'd love it." He approached a smiling clerk.

"Hello there and welcome to Salamander Resort & Spa," she said brightly. "Checking in?"

"Yes, Adam Cleary. We're here for three nights."

"Wonderful Mr. Cleary. Let me pull up your reservation. You are in luck too, as we're going to have some splendid weather this weekend, unseasonably warm."

"That's great to hear because we'll be doing some riding."

While Adam took care of all the check-in necessities, Macy wandered into the library. Its walls were paneled in dark wood bookcases, stocked to the brim with just about every kind of book you could imagine. To the left was a large hearth with a fire roaring warmly. Macy went straight to it and put her hands out; little was better than a warm fire aglow on a winter's day. Even with the unseasonably warm temperatures that were about to set in, the air was still chilly and crisp.

"Figured I'd find you in here," Adam said as he strolled up to her. "Ready to see the room?"

Their suite was magical. Again, elegant equestrian appointments were everywhere; it was a true horsemen's paradise. Adam had thoughtfully booked the Dressage Suite as he knew that was Macy's favorite riding discipline.

"So what are our plans?" Macy asked, her eyes bright. She hadn't realized how much she had been looking forward to a few days away, a break in routine was always refreshing.

"Why don't we unpack a little and then run downstairs for a quick lunch at the Gold Cup Wine Bar?"

"Sounds perfect," Macy said as she unzipped her suitcase and began sorting her items. "What about the rest of the weekend? When are we riding?" Of course, horses were also at the forefront of her mind.

"Okay, okay, I give in! Here's what we're doing. Tonight we're having dinner at The Red Fox Inn right here in town. It's one of the oldest Inns in the country, so I think you'll love reading about its history. Tomorrow we're foxhunting with the Middleburg Hunt. We're borrowing horses from my friend Jane Iverson. She and her husband, Rex, have a large estate about fifteen minutes from here, and her farm is tomorrow's fixture. The four of us are going out on their horses, and I think you'll love it, especially since you're thinking of foxhunting again.

"Tomorrow night we'll have dinner here at

Harrimans Grill, that's one of the fancier dinners. Saturday we're hitting the spa and then dinner will be at Jane's place. She's having a dinner party since I'm in town, and I thought it would be nice for you to meet some of my old friends."

Macy walked over to Adam and threw her arms around his neck, laying her head against his chest. "What an absolutely perfect weekend. I couldn't have planned it better myself."

"I was worried you'd be a little apprehensive about meeting some of my friends. Meeting friends and family is a big step, and I know you're hesitant to start a real relationship, but I can't help it. I want everyone I care about to get to know you."

Macy pulled away slightly and looked into Adam's eyes. "Then I want to get to know them too." And with a shy smile she said, "What do you say we check out the bed before heading down for lunch?"

In one swift movement, Adam scooped her up in his arms and laid her gently on the bed.

~~~~~

Lunch was splendid as a little refreshment was just what was needed after a two hour drive and a roll in the hay. They ordered off the sushi menu, splitting a few rolls and doing their best to master their chopsticks.

"I can't remember the last time I had sushi this good," commented Macy. "There was this great little place in Lexington I'd hit up on the way home from work. I was rather proficient with chopsticks; clearly I'm out of practice now." She had struggled a bit at first.

"It's a skill that if you don't use, you lose," laughed Adam. He hadn't been much better. "I'm guessing there aren't many good sushi places in our neck
~~~~~

of the woods?" As a relative newcomer to the area, Adam was still learning where to eat and what to do.

"Not really. We'd have to go into Baltimore City for some decent sushi. That's why I haven't had it since I've been home. Too far of a drive for this country mouse."

After lunch they took the quick two minute drive into downtown Middleburg, parked along E. Washington Street and strolled hand-in-hand through the many quaint shops. Of course, a stop into Middleburg Tack Exchange proved fruitful. Macy picked up a well-made second-hand Stubben bridle for Fitz. Even though he was still in rehab, so to speak, she couldn't pass up the pretty piece. *The dark brown leather will complement his dapple grey coat perfectly.*

Adam grabbed a couple used books from their large shelf. After they paid for their purchases, they walked to Cuppa Giddy Up and ordered two coffees.

As they took a table by the window so they could watch the passersby, Macy smiled. "Thank you for bringing me here. I can't believe it's been so long since I've been to Middleburg. It's very horsey, like Lexington, but it has a different, more intimate feel. It's pretty perfect."

"And just wait until you see the countryside from the back of a horse. It's breathtaking. Honestly, it was a hard decision to leave this area and move north but being close to Pimlico has been helpful."

"Did you ever think about moving to Kentucky instead? Maybe somewhere outside of Louisville so Churchill Downs could be your home track?"

"I actually did think about it and even took a few trips out there to look at farms and property nearby. But it seemed like too big of a move at the time. I liked the idea of being on the east coast and semi-close to friends down here."

“Well I for one am certainly glad you didn't move to Kentucky. Even though I will always consider it home too. I would have come back to Maryland eventually, but if my mom hadn't passed, I'm not sure I would have come home so soon." As she said that, Macy felt that familiar pang in the pit of her stomach. When she was having a good day, it was easy to forget all the bad, that Hadley wasn't just a phone call away.

Adam, sensing Macy's grief, quickly changed the subject. "After this, what do you say we swing by my old farm? A friend of mine bought it, and I told him I would be in town and might drop by. I'd like to show it off, even though it's not mine anymore."

Macy brightened at the prospect of seeing the horse farm that had meant so much to Adam. "I'd love to."

~~~~~

Just over a half hour later Adam and Macy pulled into a long tree-lined driveway. Along the road front was the familiar stone wall that both Middleburg and Lexington were known for. The main house could barely be seen from the road.

The driveway circled in front of a beautiful brick colonial, and they had no sooner gotten out of the SUV when the front door swung wide open.

"I was going to be so angry if you had come to Middleburg and hadn't stopped by!" Shouted an athletic looking man in his late forties. His hair and beard were sprinkled with grey, and he had the distinguished look of a man who lived the country life.

"I told you I'd be by!" Said a delighted Adam. The two men shook hands and then embraced in a tight
~~~~~

hug.

"And who is this beautiful young lady and why is she with you?" The man turned his attention to Macy and held out his hand.

"Brody, this is Macy Holland, my, uh, neighbor. Macy, this is Brody Mason, one of my long-time friends from the horse world."

The two shook hands and then Brody ushered them inside the house.

"Lisa's out of town visiting her sister in Florida, but she'll be back in time for Jane's dinner on Saturday."

"Great, I can't wait to see her."

The house was tastefully decorated and reminded Macy of her own home. The library to the right of the main entrance was stocked full of books of all shapes and sizes. In that room hung numerous horse show ribbons and trophies from various events. Sporting art could be found on every single wall. It was perfect.

Brody led them through the library towards the back of the house where a large country kitchen awaited them. "I'll put on some tea. You two have a seat."

"Adam how could you leave this house? It's gorgeous. And that view!" Out the kitchen windows beckoned the backyard which boasted a large red barn, riding ring, multiple fenced fields, and stately landscaping.

"It was a tough decision, that's for sure. But I needed a bit more land, and, of course, I needed to be close to a major track."

Brody sat two mugs of steaming water in front of them and passed a small box of tea bags so they could take their pick. "Here is some cream, sugar, and honey," he said, placing the small containers in front of his guests. Then he sat down to join them.

"When Adam mentioned to me that he was

thinking of moving and selling this farm, I jumped at it. I've always admired this home and property, and I was looking for a bigger place than my old one. We shook hands on it before I even had a chance to talk to Lisa about it, but I knew she'd be for it. She's always loved this place too."

"Are you in the racing industry too?" Asked Macy.

"Kind of. Not flat racing though like Adam. I train steeplechasers. When Adam has a runner who doesn't make at the track, he gives me a call. A lot of them are born jumpers and really take to steeplechasing and timber racing. I race them a bit and then some move onto third careers as foxhunters. As you can imagine, there is a huge need for fast, dependable hunters in this area."

"Do you hunt?" Asked Macy.

"Yes. Lisa and I belong to the Middleburg Hunt. She makes most of the meets; I only go out a few times a month. But I'll be going out with you two tomorrow."

"Oh that will be fun! I grew up hunting with the Elkridge-Harford Hunt, but haven't been in years. I moved to Kentucky for vet school, and only moved back to Maryland a few months ago. I have a retired racer in rehab I'm hoping to turn into my foxhunter."

After about an hour of catch up, the three took a stroll outside so Adam could show Macy the one hundred year old barn he renovated when he had owned the farm.

"I love bank barns," Macy said in awe as they entered the lower portion that had been turned into horse stalls. "They're so efficient. It's warm down here even on a cold winter's day."

While most of the horses had been turned out into their pastures for the day, two were left in recuperating from injuries. They happily munched on hay while Adam pointed out the aspects of the barn, showing Macy some of the original pieces.

"Well we'd better head back to the hotel if we're going to have time to change before dinner," Adam said after completing the tour of the barn. "Brody, thanks again for letting us drop by." The two shook hands.

"Always a pleasure, Adam. And I'm so happy I got to meet you, Macy. See you on the hunt field tomorrow."

~ Chapter 27 ~

"Right this way," said the hostess at The Red Fox Inn as she led Macy and Adam to their table at the back of the restaurant. Their table for two was situated in a private corner next to a roaring fireplace.

"The best seat in the house," said Macy as she surveyed the room and removed her coat. "Do you mind if I sit with my back to the fireplace? I'm a little chilly."

"Not at all," said Adam with the smile. "I'd probably get too hot there."

Their waitress appeared and they placed orders for two hot spiked ciders.

"I want to thank you for an absolutely wonderful day," said Macy. "But I have a feeling that tomorrow is going to be even better. I can't wait to hunt. I believe my mom hunted with Middleburg as a guest once or twice when she was younger. It might have been before I was even born, now that I think about it. She and her sister, my Aunt Cynthia, who passed away quite some time ago, spent time traveling to other hunts up and down the east coast. But she always said there was no place like home."

"She must have been quite the enthusiast."

"She really was, and she was such a good rider, a true horsewoman. It makes me happy to think that I'm getting back into it. She would have been thrilled to know that I was hunting again, especially with our club."

When the waitress brought over the spiked ciders, Macy held the hot mug in between her hands and inhaled the overwhelming scent of apples and cinnamon. "What a perfect drink on a cold day. Although Brody mentioned that it's supposed to be in the low to mid-forties tomorrow. I hope the going won't be too slick."

"I'm sure it will be okay. But just to be on the

safe side, I think we're riding second flight so we won't have to jump as much."

"Perfect because this dressage queen hasn't jumped in quite some time! That's more Erin and Molly's forte. But, of course, if I'm going to hunt regularly next season, I'd better start practicing. Erin wants me to event with her, but of course all that depends on Fitz's recovery."

When the waitress arrived with their appetizer, the baked brie wedge, Macy realized that she was starving and dived in. The mango chutney it was paired with was perfection.

Over their entrees, Adam and Macy talked with the ease of lifelong companions. Somehow being away from the painful memories at home made it easier for Macy to open up and talk more about her childhood, her parents, and her dreams for the future. She realized she didn't remember the last time she had smiled so much in one day.

~~~~~

It had been a fun, yet incredibly hectic morning. It was still dark when Adam and Macy arrived at Jane's farm, ready for the day's adventures. Jane, already in the barn and raring to go, showed them their horses for the day. Macy's mount was Chaucer, a bright bay Irish Sport Horse, and Adam would be riding, Martin, a handsome liver chestnut Oldenburg cross.

Jane's farm, Hawthorne Hill, was the fixture, so it wasn't long before the huntsman and hounds arrived and trailers began pulling in. Macy's stomach was in knots from both excitement and sheer nerves. Her face must have given her away because when Adam walked over, he put his arm around her and whispered that they'd be
~~~~~

fine.

"Jane has some of the most experienced hunters – she wouldn't put us on anything green. And, like I said, we're riding second flight, so we'll get to hang back and take it a bit easier."

"I know, you're right. It's just, I can't believe how many years it's been since I've hunted. All the sights and sounds are so familiar, yet I kind of feel like an outsider."

"Once you're in the saddle and we're moving along, it will come right back to you." Adam smiled at her and his eyes glowed warmly in the very early morning sun. He had hunted regularly when he lived in Middleburg, so he had a bit more recent experience.

The last few moments before the hunt started were chaotic. People were scrambling around trying to get ready in time; some were looking for their girths, others for a missing glove. The atmosphere was electric and Macy could feel the adrenaline charging through her veins. *How could I have stayed away from hunting for so long?* She had forgotten how contagious all of it was. When you're hunting, there really is nowhere else in the world you'd rather be.

The Master opened the meet with a few words, but Macy wasn't close enough to hear everything, and shortly thereafter, the hounds were moving off and so was first flight. She and Adam lingered a bit in the back with the others riding second flight. If they felt more comfortable throughout the day, they could move up as long as it was done safely and respectfully.

The day was more than Macy could have hoped for. Hounds opened on a line right away and off they went! As they flew through the fields at a swift gallop, Macy had never felt more alive and remembered why she had loved foxhunting so much. She smiled thinking about her mom and how happy it would make her to see her daughter having such fun at a sport she herself had adored.

For about three hours they ran across the rolling Virginia countryside, the Blue Ridge Mountains in the distance added to the bucolic backdrop. The final chase was a long one, so as other members in front of them fell behind, Macy and Adam moved up a bit. By the end of the day they had jumped a few coops, logs, and even a narrow stream. While Macy felt that her timing was a bit off, she had to admit she was proud of herself for keeping up over the fences. When they made their way back to the barn at the end, Macy was breathless and tired, but her eyes were shining. She had had the best day and only wished her mother could have been waiting back at the hunt breakfast to welcome them all in.

"So? What did you think?" Adam asked when they pulled up in front of the barn and dismounted.

"I think I'm becoming a foxhunter, stat!" Macy replied. "What an absolutely wonderful day. Thank you so much for setting it up with Jane. I can't wait to go out again. I may have to buy myself a hunter," she laughed. "I think it will be quite some time before Fitz is able to hunt, and of course Hunter is a bit too old to keep up with the field. He'd give it everything he had though."

"You could take Hunter second flight, just until you've got your legs back under you."

"You know, I might do that. He's actually never hunted, but I bet he'd love it. It would give the old man something fun to look forward to. Maybe Molly could take Traveller. As long as we stayed in the back, I think the old guys could get us around."

Excited about her new plan, Macy hummed quietly to herself as she untacked Chaucer and gave him a nice rub down. He had been a doll and was one heck of a hunter. He knew his job and loved to run, but he had listened to her the entire time. *I wonder if he's for sale?* Macy thought with an amusing smile.

After the horses were settled back in their stalls with large piles of hay, Adam and Macy joined the others at the hunt breakfast. By this time, it was well after noon, but the gathering after every hunt, regardless of time, is called a breakfast. Jane's spread was a true southern feast and Macy, famished, dived in.

"You looked like you were having a ball out there today," came a voice behind her. Macy turned around to see Brody. He handed her a cup of hot cider.

"I was having the time of my life!" said Macy, happy to see her new friend. He had ridden first flight, so she hadn't seen much of him during the hunt.

"Think you'll be back?"

"Absolutely. I can't remember the last time I've had so much fun. Now my mind is going a mile a minute thinking about getting another horse to hunt. I have an older Warmblood who was my show horse and a younger Thoroughbred who's not quite recovered from a racing injury. I think my show horse could hack me around second flight, but he's never hunted before. I don't want to overwhelm him, but he's pretty adaptable. I think my Thoroughbred will be a perfect hunter, but he's still a few weeks, if not months, from being back under saddle."

"Well, if you're serious about getting another, let me know. I always have a bunch of ex-racers I retrained for foxhunting and other disciplines. The one I was riding today is for sale as well. He's an eight year old newly ex-steeplechaser. He's only been out a handful of times, but he's taken to it like an old pro."

"Oh no, this is too tempting!" Macy laughed.

"Uh oh, what's going on?" Adam said with a grin as he walked over with a plateful of food.

"Just trying to sell her a horse," said Brody with a

wink.

"The one he was riding today is for sale. I definitely have some thinking to do. I'll give you my contact information – maybe you could send over some additional information about him?" She looked over at Adam as he started to laugh. "Don't you dare laugh – this is your fault! You brought me here, and now I'm officially hooked!"

~~~~~

"What I need is a bubble bath," sighed Macy when they got back to their room later that afternoon. The day's ride had been absolutely exhilarating, but between the physical exercise and the nerves, Macy was exhausted.

"How about I run us a both a bath?" Adam smiled wickedly. When Macy looked skeptical, he added, "and give you a back rub as well?"

"Now we're talking. My muscles are already aching!"

The bath rejuvenated the two equestrians, and they were feeling refreshed when they walked downstairs to dinner at Harriman's Grill. As they settled into their booth, they reflected on their day.

"This is the best kind of tired," noted Macy. "You know when you have a great day riding or physically working, or whatever you're doing, and you feel tired yet accomplished? It was a day well spent."

"I know exactly what you mean," said Adam. "Those are days you'll remember. Life goes so fast that only a few days stand out, you know? Everything else starts to blend together until it all blurs. Today will not be one of those days."

When their white wine arrived, Adam proposed a
~~~~~

toast. “To a perfect day riding through gorgeous countryside with the most beautiful of companions.”

“I’ll drink to that, cheers,” Macy said with a shy smile.

The meal was fabulous, but by the time dessert came, Macy could barely keep her eyes open. She was ready to hit the hay, as they say. Macy and Adam walked back to their room hand-in-hand, and while she was nervous about tomorrow being Valentine’s Day, she was finally starting to let her guard down with Adam. He had proven himself to be the good guy she’d always wanted, and she would be lying if she didn’t admit she was starting to get a little excited about their future.

~ Chapter 28 ~

Valentine's Day began with breakfast in bed, which was something that made Macy very happy. She was so sore from riding the day before that she could barely move. Not having to get dressed to go downstairs and grab something to eat was marvelous. Already Adam was winning at this holiday.

"Our spa appointments start at eleven o'clock," Adam said as they lingered in bed drinking their coffee and chatting about the day ahead. "We're both starting with the hydrotherapy and getting massages. Not a couples' massage though, I figured you'd hate that," said Adam.

Macy laughed. "You're right, I would hate that, sorry. But a massage today sounds heavenly. I can't believe how sore I am. I ride regularly – my muscles shouldn't ache this much."

"True, but you don't gallop and jump regularly. And I'm sure you tensed up periodically, that doesn't help."

"You're right. Every time we came to a jump, I definitely tensed. But once we sailed over, I was like, why was I so worried about that?"

"You just need to jump more, that's all. Then you'll be flying over four-foot oxers without batting an eyelash."

"Not so sure about that!" Macy laughed. She may have jumped four feet back in the day, but she was pretty sure those days were long gone. That's what you did when you were young and brave and slightly stupid.

A few hours later, Macy and Adam walked back into their room and collapsed on their bed. The spa treatments had been divine.

"I really needed that," sighed Macy. "Thank you so much for scheduling that massage. I'm so relaxed now that I think I could sleep for a month."

Adam, tired yet happy as well, pulled Macy close to him and within a few moments, both were fast asleep.

~~~~~

"Well don't you two make a handsome couple," said an elegant woman waltzing in Macy and Adam's direction.

They had arrived at Jane's farm for the dinner party, and while Macy was looking forward to the evening, she was nervous to meet Adam's friends.

"Lisa, you look amazing," said Adam as he embraced the beautiful woman.

"Lisa, I'd like you to meet Macy. Macy, this is Lisa, Brody's wife." Lisa gave Macy a warm hug and guided them both to the bar for some cocktails.

"Brody tells me you're a veterinarian – how useful for you Adam!" Lisa laughed. "You two could make quite the team," she said with a slick smile.

Brody joined them a moment later and the three of them filled Lisa in on the morning's foxhunting adventures.

"I'm sorry to have missed it," said Lisa. "My flight got in around noon, so Brody was home, had the horse up, and was showered by the time I pulled in the drive."

Jane appeared shortly thereafter and hugged each of her guests. "I'm so happy to have you all here tonight. Adam, you have no idea how much we've missed you. To have you home, and to meet darling Macy, has just been such a treat."

"It's great to be back. I hadn't realized how much
~~~~~

I've missed everyone too – and the area. Middleburg is so similar to where we are in Maryland, yet it's different, of course. No beautiful Blue Ridge Mountains in Maryland."

"Well maybe they can help lure you back," Jane said with a sly smile.

"I think today's hunt may have helped lure Macy here," Brody said. "I know you have your hunts up your way, but ours are simply the best."

"No bias there!" Adam laughed.

"Well, let's head into dinner. I think the table is set now. We can continue our conversation, and our plan to bring Adam home, in here," laughed Jane as she ushered her guests into the elegantly-appointed dining room.

An avid collector of sporting art, Macy was enchanted by the work which decorated the room. Two Franklin Vosses flanked the large stone fireplace that anchored the room. Voss, a well-known equestrian painter in the early twentieth century, still has roots in Maryland.

Macy, sitting next to Jane, told her so. "Franklin Voss actually lived in Monkton, about three or four miles from where Adam and I live now. His brother, Edward, owned Atlanta Hall, a gorgeous farm that's still in the Voss family today. Now it's a breeding and training facility; the owner trains both flat racers and steeplechasers. And most of the family hunts with Elkridge-Harford."

"Isn't that fascinating? I had heard of Atlanta Hall but didn't realize it was in Monkton. Adam, maybe I won't be able to lure you home after all! I haven't been up that way in years, but I do know that the countryside is breathtaking."

"So you've been to Monkton?" asked Macy.

"Yes, I actually hunted with your club as a guest many years ago, probably 20 or 25 years now. I do remember being completely enraptured with the area."

The evening was simply splendid. There were fourteen guests in total, all equestrians, so naturally horses were the main topic of conversation. Dinner was delicious, and the pecan pie for dessert was exceptional. Macy wanted to ask for a second helping, but she didn't want to look like a glutton!

After dinner, cocktails and brandy were served in the library, which Macy decided was her favorite room in the house. It reminded her of her own, a cozy room with floor-to-ceiling bookshelves lined with every type of book imaginable. Of course, Jane's library was larger in size as it comfortably fit all fourteen guests.

This room also had a stone fireplace complete with a roaring fire, and Macy happily sat across from it, feeling the warmth on her face.

"Having a good time?" asked Adam as he sidled up next to her.

"Yes, I am. Your friends are lovely. Jane is amazing – I can see why you love them all so much."

"She's really pushing to get me to come back. I can't leave Maryland though – being so close to Pimlico and Laurel is such an advantage. And living next door to you isn't so bad either." He leaned in and gave Macy the softest of kisses. "Thank you for coming here with me. It means a lot to me that you get to know my friends. I don't have a lot of family; these people are my family."

"I'm honored to get to know them. If they're special to you, they're special to me too."

~ Chapter 29 ~

"Sounds like you had a great time," said Erin as she prepared a salad for the two to share for dinner. She expertly chopped up the grilled chicken to be added on top.

"It really was. I was surprised at how much I actually enjoyed myself. It's always a big step in the relationship when you meet the other person's friends, so I kind of thought I'd freeze up and withdraw, but that wasn't the case at all. I found myself really hoping they'd like me."

"It doesn't hurt that they're all horse people too – you had plenty in common. Horses make life so easy, don't they? When in doubt when you don't know what to say to a new person, talk horses."

"That's true. You would have liked them all as well, Jane especially. I think Adam said she's about seventy years old, but you'd never know it. She outrode me in the field, flying over logs and streams as if it was nothing. That's exactly how I want to be when I'm that age, still riding – still active."

"Me too. Don't you love that our sport is one you can do for an entire lifetime?"

"Absolutely. Horses keep you going, that's for sure." Macy finished setting the table and went to the fridge. "Do you want a vinaigrette, olive oil, or Ranch dressing?"

"Silly question. Ranch of course." The two laughed as Macy put the Ranch on the table and filled two glasses with water.

"So do you think marriage is on the horizon for you two?" Erin asked with the smirk as they sat down to eat.

"My goodness no! I'll admit, I did like being introduced as his girlfriend, which he did at Jane's dinner, but I think I'll be more than happy with that for quite some time."

"I'm just happy you're coming around. I know you two had a rocky start, and of course you had so much going on personally, but I think Adam's one of the good ones. I'm glad you're giving the relationship a chance."

"Me too. I wouldn't have said that a few months ago, but I'm happy too. Now we just need to find you a new man!"

"Never!" Erin laughed as she tossed a roll in Macy's direction. "Well maybe eventually. Right now I'll live vicariously through you and Molly."

"Speaking of Molly, she's such a good party planner. She has completely taken the reins with planning Cora's baby shower, for which I'm so grateful. I just haven't had the time to think about it. It's so sweet of your mom to host us."

"Of course. Mom's excited for Tommy and Cora's baby too. Lord knows she's never getting a grandchild from me! Molly and Beau will give her one, but probably not for another year or two. Mom wants a little one to spoil."

"Well Cora can't wait. Tommy, he'll be hanging out in the den watching sports with your dad! Cora told him he needs to be on hand for pictures, but he didn't need to sit there while she opened gifts."

"I was at the tack shop the other day and got her this cute onesie. It says, "I'm here, now where's my pony?" I know Cora doesn't ride, but I know you'll make sure this little one does."

"That sounds adorable! And you're right – any Holland from here and out will grow up riding, or else!"

~~~~~

The Sorrenson's house was bathed in pink. Balloons, streamers, and all other baby shower décor conceivable filled just about every room on the main level. Cora had recently found out she was having a little girl. Their initial plan was to wait until the birth and be surprised, but they changed their minds. Tommy called Macy after Cora's last doctor's appointment to give her the big news. Now it was the end of February, and Cora had about two and a half months to go.

The mom-to-be arrived looking resplendent in an attractive dress and low-heeled boots. Macy admired her sister-in-law for she was still stylish and fashionable at seven months pregnant.

After greeting and hugging all the guests, Tommy made his way to the kitchen where Macy and Molly were putting the finishing touches on the food.

"Grab yourself some something to eat," said Molly, handing Tommy a plate.

"Don't mind if I do. Then I'm going to disappear. Call me when the cake's out!" Tommy filled his plate, gave his sister a quick kiss on the cheek, and headed into the den with Molly's father.

The shower was perfect. Cora's friends and family filled the family room and watched happily as she opened present after present. Of course, quite a few of them were horse-themed, which excited Macy. She couldn't wait to spoil her little niece and hoped that she would be a horse lover.

As Macy glanced around the room, it pained her that her mom wasn't there. She was missing out on so many wonderful occasions. There were so many future memories she wouldn't be a part of.

As if sensing Macy's sadness, Molly reached over
~~~~~

and rubbed her friend's back. Molly gave Macy a little wink, and Macy returned it with a grin. Thank goodness for friends.

"Do you and Tommy have any names picked out?" asked Karen.

"Yes, actually we just decided, so you all will be the first to know. We've decided on Elizabeth. That was Hadley's middle name." Cora, tears in her eyes, smiled at Macy and the two girls got up to embrace.

"Mom would have been so honored. Thank you," Macy choked out. She couldn't say more than that without all-out sobbing.

After they sat back down and Cora finished with her presents, Erin declared that it was time to cut the cake! Tommy had been summoned and the happy couple stood behind the pink-frosted cake, smiling for endless photos.

Later that evening after the guests had left, Macy stayed behind to help Karen clean up.

"Elizabeth Leigh Holland. What a beautiful name and a wonderful tribute to your mother," said Karen as she wiped down the kitchen counters.

"Your mom would have been so happy," said Molly. "A part of her will live on."

"And Leigh is Cora's middle name, right?" asked Erin.

"Yep," answered Macy. "And Cora said they'll probably call her Beth. I think that's cute."

"I'm not going to lie, seeing Cora all glowing and seeing those adorable outfits totally gave me baby fever!" cried Molly.

Erin rolled her eyes at that one, but Karen clapped her hands. "Get to it Molly!"

"Well I'm still not completely ready, but maybe in another year or so. I think Beau's ready now."

“Gag me,” said Erin, but with a smile. She liked the idea of being an aunt, just not a mom.

A short time later the house was back to normal. The food had been put away, the decorations had come down, and the balloons pushed into the corner of the family room.

As Macy put on her coat, preparing to leave, she hugged Karen tightly. “Again, I can’t thank you enough for what you’ve done and continue to do for my family. I wouldn’t have made it through these past few months without you.” Tears sprang into Macy’s eyes and Karen pulled her into another embrace.

“Yes, you could have, honey. You’re a strong young lady. But we’re happy to be here for you. We love you.”

~ Chapter 30 ~

As is typical of Maryland winters, March came in like a lion. On March 1st, to be exact, Macy and Erin hunkered down inside while a blizzard raged. With a foot on the ground already and another foot expected, the girls did what most people do when trapped inside by Mother Nature – they baked.

Chocolate chip cookies were cooling on the rack. Apple crisp was in the oven, and Macy sat flipping through a cookbook looking for the perfect soup recipe.

"I'd love some cream of crab soup right now, but unfortunately we're fresh out of crab."

"We didn't prepare well enough for this storm, I guess," said Erin, who was sipping some chardonnay and getting ready to sample a cookie.

"Maybe I'll just go with the classic chicken noodle."

"These cookies are delicious," said Erin after a big bite. "If you're definitely making soup, I'll make some bread."

"Perfect. I think I'm going to invite Adam over too."

"Good idea. Can I give Julep a small piece of cookie? She's begging so beautifully."

Macy laughed. The greedy little dog had perfected her begging face. "Yes, a small piece, not too many chocolate chips."

She texted Adam.

Macy: Want to join us for dinner? Chicken noodle soup.
Adam: Yes, thank you. What should I bring?
Macy: Nothing! We've been baking all day. See you at 6?
Adam: Can't wait.

Things with Adam had been going really well, and Macy worried that things were going too well. She didn't know why, but she felt like she was waiting for the bottom to fall out.

Adam had been busy with his big Derby horse. Etch had been shipped to Florida where he was training and was being prepped for the Florida Derby later in the month. The trail to the Kentucky Derby had begun in earnest, and Adam was consumed by it. Macy, excited by Etch's chances of doing well, also caught the horseracing bug.

"Adam's coming for dinner. I told him to be here at six o'clock," Macy mentioned to Erin, who was pulling the ingredients for homemade bread from the refrigerator and cupboard.

"Sounds good. It'll be nice to catch up. I have some ideas about Jazzy's training I'd like to run by him."

"Speaking of training, I can't wait for this snow to get out of here and for the warm weather. Fitz's basically full-rehabbed now – it's time to get to get in his saddle and get moving."

"Do you think he'll be able to physically withstand being a foxhunter? That's what you want to do with him, right?"

"Yes, ideally I'd like to hunt with him. I will do one last set of follow up x-rays, and probably have Beau give him a once-over too to see if I'm missing anything, but he should be 100% when it's all said and done. Of course, I'll listen to Fitz and let him tell me what he can do and how far he can go, so we shall see!"

Macy was excited about the prospect of getting Fitz back into shape. As a former racehorse, he already knew the basics, so it would just be a matter of retraining him for another discipline. She'd start slow with just lots of walking and gradually build him up to trotting. Getting him in shape was the first order of business. At that point, she'd re-evaluate, see where they were, and then, hopefully, start taking him over some cavaletti and tiny fences much later in the year.

"I'm really looking forward to working with him. It's nice to have a project – something to keep me focused," she said to Erin.

"Hear, hear. You know I'm right there with you. Jazzy is a lifesaver right now. With the divorce and work extra crazy at the moment, it's nice to come home, see Jazz, and just think about her for a bit. Horses are so amazing, aren't they? They demand 100% of your attention, so it's impossible to think about all of life's problems when you're with them."

"You're right about that. I don't know what I would have done during vet school and then my internship – heck, life in general – if it hadn't been for Hunter. That horse is everything to me."

The girls got busy preparing dinner and soon the aroma of a hearty chicken noodle soup, buttery bread, and hot chocolate filled the house. When Adam walked in through the back door, he took a deep breath.

"Smells amazing, ladies! Thanks for having me over," he said as an excited Mint Julep went flying into his arms.

After snuggling Julep for a moment, he placed her back on the floor so he could take off his hat, coat, and snow boots. The girls had gone out about an hour before to feed the horses, and there had been about a foot and a half of snow by then.

"It's still really coming down," Adam said as he walked over and gave Macy a kiss. "I think it's supposed to snow through the night."

The girls groaned. Snow was fun, and as

Marylanders, they were used to it, but by the time March came everyone was over winter and ready for spring.

"Beau's on call tonight," Macy said while finishing setting the table. "I hope everything stays quiet for him. He'll have a terrible time getting out." Beau's truck was a heavy duty diesel, but still. Venturing out in a snowstorm was never fun.

Dinner was wonderful. Even Erin remarked how amazing it was that something so simple like chicken noodle soup could be so perfect. They had made plenty of it, so each went back for seconds and thirds. Even little Julep got a few bites of chicken and bread added to her regular dinner of kibble.

They talked about everything: training schedules for Jazzy and Fitz, Etch and his next race, the odds of him earning enough points to qualify for the Kentucky Derby, and of course, the miserable weather.

After dinner they settled into the library next to a blazing fire, their mugs of hot chocolate topped off with thick homemade whipped cream. Julep curled up on the rug in front of the fire and was out like a light. It was a picture perfect evening.

"When do you leave for Florida?" Macy asked. She and Adam were lounging together on the couch while Erin dozed in the chair next to the fire. Macy laughed softly as both Julep and Erin snored quietly.

"Next week. I have two horses coming here for lay-ups. Minor injuries, but they'll be out of training for a bit, and I need the room at Pimlico for two other trainees coming up from Florida. I'll get the lay-ups settled in, then I'll head to Florida myself. Gil will be staying at the farm looking after everyone. Gil was one of Adam's most trusted grooms.

"I'll miss you while you're gone," said Macy, and she found that she really meant it. She and Adam were growing closer, but the thought of that didn't scare her as much as it used to.

"I'll miss you too. I'll be thinking of you the whole time," he said as he leaned in to kiss Macy. It was slow and passionate and full of the warmth she felt for him.

"Want to go upstairs?" Macy whispered with a devilish grin.

"You read my mind."

~ Chapter 31 ~

"Easy boy, nice and easy," Macy said softly as she led Fitz over to the mounting block. Fitz's x-rays had come back perfectly when Beau had visited earlier in the week, so Macy was finally clear to start riding him again. "Take it slow," Beau had cautioned. "Lots and lots of walking. He's out of shape and coming back from an injury. Just walk – and when you've grown bored of that, walk some more."

Macy had laughed, but of course she knew she had to bring Fitz back inch by inch. The last thing she wanted to do was rush this portion of his training and land them back at square one.

There was a small, flat paddock next to the barn that Macy had been using as her ring. While it was grass and not sand, it was small enough that Fitz couldn't really get himself going into a gallop if he decided to act like a fool. The first two times Macy had ridden him, he'd been great.

Today was a bit breezy, so Fitz snorted at the shadows dancing from the nearby trees. Macy whispered quietly to him and he calmed down.

They had made a few turns around the paddock when Erin appeared, Jazzy in tow.

"Want some company?" Erin asked.

"Sure," replied Macy. Fitz and Jazzy were friends now, (as much as Jazzy was friends with anyone), and it would do the youngsters well to learn how to work with distractions.

After Erin mounted up, she and Jazzy walked alongside Macy and Fitz, giving them a wide berth in case either horse acted up. Both of them walked quietly together as if they had done it for years.

"I guess Adam is thrilled with Etch's latest victory. The Florida Derby is a huge prep race. Do they have enough points to enter the Kentucky Derby?" Asked Erin.

"He is on cloud nine. It was such a decisive win too – he couldn't be prouder of Etch. I'm not sure but if he doesn't have enough points, he's awfully close. This is so exciting, isn't it? I love horseracing."

"Me too. And to think we met a Derby contender – pretty cool."

The girls continued to walk for a few more minutes until Erin put Jazzy through her paces. As she was in regular work with no restrictions, Erin trotted and cantered the mare around the paddock. She made sure to give Fitz plenty of space, but he took everything in stride. He got a little jumpy once when Erin cantered up behind him, even though she called out to remind him that she was there, but he settled quickly.

"I'm sure he remembers his racing days. When a horse comes up behind him, that means dig deeper and go!" Macy laughed. Fitz would figure it all out in time. Retraining for a new career off the track took time. Luckily, Macy was in no rush. She wanted to make sure Fitz's retraining went as smoothly as possible.

After Erin had finished with Jazzy's workout, she brought the mare alongside Fitz again for a leisurely cool out.

"So what are your plans for Jazzy this season? Will you take her to any shows?"

"Yes, I actually have a few tentatively on the calendar. Of course, I want to take it slow, but I figured a few schooling shows would be great exposure."

"Are you still planning to event her?"

"Absolutely," Erin said with a huge grin. Eventing had been Erin's main focus for years having left the hunter world behind by the time she reached high school. Unlike Molly and Macy, who were excellent, confident riders, Erin was simply fearless. She didn't bat an eye at the monstrous jumps horses and riders needed to sail over in the upper levels of eventing. Macy and Molly always admired her ability take massive log and table jumps with ease.

"Where will you start?"

"There's a dressage schooling show at Olney in May that I think would be a good intro into the world of showing. Who knows how she'll react. Before I take her there though, I'll probably trailer her off the farm and school at Tranquillity a few times just so she gets used to working in new places."

"Those Maryland Dressage Association schooling shows are the best," Macy said with a wink. As she was the dressage aficionado, of course she'd approve of Erin starting her horse there. "And Tranquillity is perfect too, especially since they have multiple rings. You could probably work her in relative quiet but still feel confident that she's seeing a bit of the hustle and bustle that comes with being off the farm."

"I think Molly is going to take Gypsy to the same shows, as long as these babies keep progressing as well as they have been," she said with a smile as she lovingly rubbed Jazzy's silky neck. "Later this summer I might take her to a low level jumper show, or maybe even a CT. She won't be ready for cross country this year, but she could probably pop over some tiny fences in a ring."

All this talk just excited Macy. Fitz would miss the entire show season as she rehabbed him back into work, but she didn't care. She'd tag along with Molly and Erin and help them on show days. And maybe one day she'd get out there with Fitz. Of course, she was still really hoping that Fitz would turn out to be her foxhunting prospect, but she'd wait and let him tell her what he wanted to do.

"Will you take Hunter out at all? I know he's semi-retired and these low level shows are beneath our FEI award-winning Hunter, but it might be fun!"

"They are not beneath us!" Macy exclaimed. "You know, I don't have any plans, but I'm sure he'd love to get out. He hasn't had a job, other than being my very spoiled pet, in quite some time." Macy had always loved competing with Hunter. From the very beginning of their partnership, he had known he was a star. He put his game face on, walked into the ring like he owned it, and dominated. For years, they were unstoppable.

"Well, we have a fun show season to look forward to, and who knows, maybe by the fall you can take Fitz out after all," said Erin.

"You know, I definitely don't want to get ahead of myself, but I'd love to get him out too. I'm sure he'd enjoy it. Horses like having jobs, especially Thoroughbreds."

"That they do – which is why I will never own another breed," smiled Erin.

Macy smiled back. Even though she would always be a huge fan of Warmbloods like Hunter, she had grown up riding Thoroughbreds too and knew them to be willing, athletic animals who put their heart and soul into their work.

She was also happy to see Erin so content. They both had had a lot on their plates for quite some time, so these project horses could not have come at a better time.

~ Chapter 32 ~

"Winner, chicken dinner!" Trilled Macy when Adam opened the door. She had walked over when he got home from Florida to congratulate him in person on Etch's victory in the Florida Derby. This horse was really going places, and she couldn't be happier for Adam and all of the horse's connections.

Adam scooped Macy up into a bear hug and spun her around.

"So, how does it feel to have the top Derby contender?" Macy asked.

Adam popped a quick kiss on her forehead and said, "It feels exciting, but incredibly nerve-wracking. As you know with horses, anything can go wrong at any time. Now we're just focused on keeping him happy and healthy."

Macy knew that to be the absolute truth. Horses are the most unpredictable animals and also accident prone. A slip here, a stray kick into a fence there, and the next thing you know you have an unsound horse that needs time off to heal and recover. Fitz was a prime example.

A noise in the driveway made Macy turn around. "Expecting company?"

"Yes, I have a lay-up coming in today. Bowed tendon. She's going to stay here and recuperate. Want to help me settle her into her stall?"

"Of course."

One of Adam's assistants, Gil, expertly backed the trailer down the driveway as close to the barn as he could get. As soon as she neared the barn, however, Macy could tell something was wrong. She heard banging coming from one of the stalls, and she and Adam sprinted over as quickly as they could.

"Shit, it's Piper. Looks like he's cast. Get Gil in here quick – he can help us move him."

Macy took off back out of the barn and shouted for Gil. A horse getting cast, or stuck, essentially, in their stall can be devastating. If they accidentally lay too close to the wall of their stall, wedging themselves in so tight that they can't get back up, they will panic and thrash around, potentially injuring themselves. Macy had seen too many cast horses who had needed to be put down because of broken legs. Thank goodness Gil was here – another pair of hands would be necessary.

Adam was hovering over the horse, speaking softly, trying to calm him down and prevent him from hurting himself. Piper was completely lathered up with sweat dripping off his body. Macy knew that the best way to help a cast horse was to stand behind him, grab his mane and neck area, and pull him towards the center of the stall. This allows him to free his legs and hopefully right himself on his own.

The three of them gathered behind Piper's neck, took hold, and pulled with all their might. Even three people isn't much of a match for a crazed horse, but bit by bit, they were able to move him close enough to the center that he was able to straighten his legs.

It took him a moment or two, but Piper gathered his legs under him, pushed up, and stood. As soon as he was up, Macy knew something was wrong. The horse was favoring his right front leg, limping on it as he tried to move around. She could tell that the injury was high on the leg, somewhere just below the shoulder.

"Shit," she muttered as she went towards him. Adam was already haltering the poor, traumatized horse, and Macy instructed Adam not to move him.

"I need to run back to the house and get my truck.

We'll sedate him and take some x-rays." She sprinted out of the stall before Adam could respond and ran back to her house.

Inside the house she grabbed her truck keys, jumped in the driver's seat, and gunned it out of there. Every minute counted in a situation like this. The more the horse moved around on his injury, the more damage he'd do. She needed to get there quickly, administer pain meds, and sedate him.

By the time Macy got back to Piper's stall, she could see that the horse wasn't in good shape. He was still sweating profusely and was clearly exhausted from the whole ordeal. She could see that it was taking everything to keep him on his feet – Adam was practically holding him up. Gil had settled the new horse into her stall and was back beside Piper, talking quietly, soothing the animal.

Macy immediately injected the horse with some meds and was running back to the truck for the portable x-ray machine when she realized that Beau had borrowed it. They only had one between them and now she remembered that he had taken it just last week after he'd x-rayed Fitz. She shot off a quick call to him; thankfully, he was only about fifteen minutes out and would be there soon.

Macy felt tears sting her eyes. This was the part of her job that she hated – seeing an animal in pain and not being able to do much about it. Her gut told her that they were dealing with a fracture, and if that was the case, there wasn't much that could be done. If it was a clean break, he may have a chance of survival, but if the bone has shattered, this would be his last day.

His last day. The tears came, but Macy wiped them away. She had a job to do and the horse was counting on her.

Not long after, Macy heard Beau's truck flying down the driveway – he skidded to a stop right in front of her. The truck wasn't even in park before Macy was opening the hatch in the back, searching for the machine.

Together she and Beau moved in unison. If it hadn't been such a horrifying experience, watching the horse begin to shake from its pain, Macy would have been reminded about some of the old days where they worked on emergencies at Rood & Riddle in Lexington.

Macy let Beau take the lead since he had used this particular machine more than she had. Within a few minutes the worst was confirmed.

"Multiple fractures," said Beau with a frown. These were the days he hated the most too.

"What are his chances?" Asked Adam, his voice serious and drained.

"We could rush him up to New Bolton for surgery. I'd say chance of a successful outcome there is around 30% at best. After that, chances of a recovery where he has any real quality of life, probably less than 10%. Arthritis will set in eventually, if he makes it that far." Beau sighed heavily. "If he were mine, I'd put him down right now."

"Let me call his owner. I'd like his permission first. If I can't get a hold of him, then we'll do it anyway. I won't let him suffer." As Adam walked out of the stall, Macy could see tears in his eyes as well.

"So you think surgery is an option though? Maybe we should try it," Macy said to Beau, panic rising in her voice.

"Mace, you know as well as I do that there's not much we can do for this horse. You know I'm an advocate for surgery – but only when it makes sense. It doesn't here. We'd be subjecting this horse to a life of chronic pain, if he even makes it through the surgery."

"I know, I guess I was just hoping for a miracle."

"I know you were. I was too. I can't stand this anymore than you can."

Adam walked back in. "I have the owner's permission. He says to go ahead."

With that Beau walked back out to his truck to prepare the lethal injection. Macy stood by Piper's head and soothed him, kissed his nose, and told him that he was such a wonderful boy. Adam walked over too and gave the horse a last pat. He had enjoyed training this one, he'd been willing and eager to please.

"Rest easy, sweet boy. We're so sorry it had to end like this. We love you," said Macy with tears streaming down her cheeks.

She handed the lead to Adam as Beau came over and took his place by Piper's neck.

Macy, unable to handle the scene that was about to unfold, walked out of the barn, got into her truck, and drove away.

~ Chapter 33 ~

It was almost dark by the time she got home. After leaving Adam's Macy just drove. Up and down the backroads, out in the country. She just wanted to get lost. Both Erin and Adam had called her multiple times, so she knew she'd better go home before anyone worried too much.

When she parked in front of the house, she saw Adam's SUV in her drive. He had been sitting on her porch waiting for her.

"I'm so sorry about your horse," was all she said.

"Thanks. He was one of the good ones. An easy, fun ride, and a character at the barn. Everyone loved him," he said with a sad sniff. Macy had to remember that she wasn't the only one grieving. Adam had known the horse far longer than she had.

"I'm sorry I ran out like that. I just couldn't see it. I can't tell you how many horses I've put down in my career so far, one only two days ago, but today. I just couldn't do it. I would have had Beau not been there, but – I guess I just needed to run."

"You know I understand, but next time, run to me." With that, he stood up and held out his arms for her, but Macy couldn't move. She felt like her feet were stuck in concrete.

"Is this all life is? Just sadness? Just one loss after another?"

Adam dropped his arms and walked over to her. "Sometimes, yes. Especially in our professions. You know what it's like to deal with thousand pound, accident prone animals every single day. Things like this happen. This kind of stuff, it's out of our control, but it's no one's fault."

"Well maybe I'm in the wrong profession. Maybe I'm in the wrong life."

"Mace, don't say that," Adam said as he tried to wrap her in his arms.

"Please Adam, no," she said as she wiggled out of his grasp. "I'm sorry, but I just need some space." She unlocked the door and walked into the dark house.

~~~~~

The following day was warm and relentlessly sunny. While Macy loved sunshine, she also liked it when the weather reflected her mood. Today should have been rainy and gloomy.

She had Fitz in crossties in the middle of the aisle and was giving him a good grooming when she heard a truck pull up outside.

"Anyone home?" It was Beau.

"Hey, Beau, in here."

The tall, lean man who had become one of her best friends walked down the aisle and put his hand on Fitz's neck. The grey horse batted Beau's shoulder with his nose, and Beau returned the gesture with a good scratch on Fitz's withers. "So, want to tell me what happened yesterday?" He asked sadly. He knew Macy still wasn't herself, but yesterday's blow up had caught him off guard. It was obvious his friend was still hurting.

"Beau, I honestly don't know." Macy sighed as she tossed her dandy brush back in the caddy and grabbed a tail comb. "I don't know. I just lost it. This poor horse – he had the brightest future – and it's all gone just because he got stuck in his stall. It's all…so senseless."

"I know. It's hard and it hurts, but this is what we do, Mace. Sometimes we have to make these decisions. Sometimes we have to let them go." His voice was kind
~~~~~

and soft.

"I'm just so tired of death. I mean, I had just put a horse down the other day – it wasn't like I hadn't done this recently. It wasn't like I hadn't seen suffering. I'm just tired of it. I guess this one was just the straw that broke the camel's back."

"Death is part of the job, Mace, you know that. I don't like it any more than you do, but there's not much we can do about it. I know it hurts like hell, but we ended his suffering. That's the kindest thing we can do."

"You're completely right, I know that. And I want you to know that had you not been there, I wouldn't have run away. I wouldn't have left that horse. But," she paused as her chin began to tremble. "I guess this one just caught me off guard. I honestly can't explain my behavior, but Beau, I am so sorry. It was unacceptable of me take off the way I did."

"I know you wouldn't have left an animal in need, Mace, don't give that a second thought. I'm just worried about you. What do you need? Would you like some time off? I can spare you for a little bit. If you need some time – take it. Do whatever you have to do to feel better."

"I appreciate the offer Beau, but no, I don't need any time off. Actually, I've found that it's been better if I stay busy. Too much free time isn't good for this girl – I don't need any more time to think," she said with a smirk. "The less I think about anything, the better off everyone is."

"Well you're still planning to go to Kentucky in a bit to help Cassidy move, right?"

"Yes, if that's okay. That's still the plan."

"It's fine. Take as long as you need to help her settle in. A few days away from here will do you some good."

"Thanks Beau. I know Cassidy caused you a

bunch of trouble, so I appreciate you not having a problem with our friendship."

"All that's in the past. I wish Cass nothing but the best. I'm sure she'll be great at New Bolton." He paused to greet Julep as she came barreling down the aisle. "Hey girl! Where have you been? Your paws are all muddy."

"Chasing mice and rats in the fields, I bet," Macy said with a smile. She loved that little rascal.

"Well I best get on out of here. Molly and I have a date night tonight."

"Oh fun! Tell her I'll return her call tomorrow. I'm sure she was worried when I went MIA yesterday."

"She was, but she figured you were out taking a drive."

Macy gave a soft laugh. "That girl knows me too well. Thanks for coming by and checking on me, Beau. Again, I'm really sorry about my behavior yesterday. You're a good boss and an even better friend. Thanks for putting up with me."

Beau walked over and pulled Macy into a tight hug. "Don't mention it."

As he started back up the aisle, he turned around. "Hey, after you left yesterday, Adam seemed to think that you were angry at him. It was a tense situation, but he was in a tough spot. At the end of the day, he has to listen to his owners. It sucks, but those aren't his horses. But even still, putting that horse down was the right thing to do."

"I know it was. I was upset, but not at him."

"Good. Hopefully you two had a chance to talk."

~ Chapter 34 ~

"Thank you so much for coming to help me!" Cassidy squealed as she threw her arms around Macy. The two girls were standing outside the Louisville airport where Cassidy had come to meet Macy's plane.

"Of course! And this is purely selfish – I'm excited to have you closer to me. Only an hour away!"

They quickly grabbed Macy's luggage and put it in the back of Cassidy's pickup truck, and then hit the road southeast into Lexington. Macy was going to help Cassidy finish packing up her apartment and then drive with her to Pennsylvania.

"I was nervous about how I'd feel coming back here, but it feels nice, like home," said Macy with a sigh of relief.

"You haven't been back since you left Rood and Riddle, right?"

"Yep, I quit, packed up, found a company to haul Hunter and Fitz, and was out of here without a backward glance. I always felt that I'd go back home but not exactly under those circumstances."

"Life is crazy, isn't it? You never know what it's going to throw at you. I never thought I'd leave. This is the only home I've ever known. My parents are pissed."

"Well they can visit any time. And this is a huge step forward in your career; they've got to be proud of you for that."

"Proud isn't a word my parents throw around often," Cass said with an eyeroll. "They understand, sort of. But the other day my dad offered to buy me a house if I stayed. Can you believe that?"

"Wow! That's quite an offer. Must be nice!"

"It was their last act of desperation. But that house

would have come with so many conditions – it wasn't worth it. They think money can buy everything, and it can buy a whole hell of a lot, but it can't buy me. Not anymore. When I was younger I might have taken them up on it, but not now. I need to make a life for myself that doesn't involve them."

"Good for you. Besides, you'll love New Bolton, and you'll love Chester County. It's not too far over the Maryland line and is gorgeous east coast horse country.

"I'm excited for a new adventure," Cass said with a smile. "And maybe I'll even meet a guy! I'm getting pretty tired of living the single life. And speaking of guys, how's yours?"

Macy hesitated. "Well, things are…well I'm not really sure how we are. I didn't leave things too pretty before I left."

"That doesn't sound good. What happened?"

As the girls sped along towards Lexington and Cassidy's apartment, Macy filled her friend on the latest. She told her about Piper getting cast and him having to be put down. She told Cass how she just lost it and took off, leaving poor Adam to handle everything on his own.

"I know it wasn't Adam's fault and that he wasn't left with much of a choice, but still. Like I told Beau, the whole scenario was just the straw that broke the camel's back. It was a reminder that life isn't fair – that sometimes it really sucks. It kind of pushed me over the edge again, so I told Adam that I just needed a little space. We haven't talked much since then. I went over to his house last night to tell him I was heading here in the morning, and we talked, but we didn't really resolve anything. I still just said I needed space. He understood."

"So, you're breaking up?"

"No, not exactly. I'm not sure what we're doing. I guess we need to talk some more, but I didn't have it in me to hash it all out then. I don't want to break up, but I don't know what I want. Besides, he's got enough on his mind. Etch is the Derby favorite – you knew that, right? Adam's actually on his way to Kentucky tomorrow."

"I did – so exciting! Hopefully you guys will get a chance to talk before too long. He sounds like such a great guy – I'd hate to see you two end it before it's really had a chance to start."

Macy sighed loudly. "I agree with you completely."

~~~~~

The following day Macy and Cassidy sat in the living room surrounded by mounds of boxes. Each was labeled with its contents and appropriate room. The number of books she'd collected over the years was pretty unreal.

"These are so heavy," Macy said as she pushed a box filled to the brim with books with her foot.

"Let's leave the heavier ones for the movers," Cass laughed. "The lightweight ones and must-haves we'll take with us in the truck." She surveyed the room. "Honestly, I'm shocked I have so much stuff. You wouldn't believe all the bags and bags I have already given to Red Cross. I'm glad I did that or else we'd really be in trouble."

"I did the same thing when I left and still couldn't believe how much junk I did pack. When I got back to Maryland and unpacked, I threw even more stuff out." Macy's phone binged alerting her to a text message.

"I just got a text from Adam. He's in Kentucky and wants to meet up tomorrow."

"Meet him! I have my farewell luncheon anyway – meet him then. You are, of course, still invited to come
~~~~~

with me, but I know you said you'd rather skip it."

"Yeah, I didn't leave on the best of terms. Probably best I steer clear," she said with a sad smile. "Okay, I'll tell Adam I'll meet him. I do miss him."

~ Chapter 35 ~

It was an absolutely gorgeous early May afternoon when Macy pulled up in front of the Windy Corner Café. There wasn't a cloud in the sky. Macy and Adam had agreed on a late lunch, so the parking lot was virtually empty as she pulled in driving Cassidy's truck. She didn't see Adam, so she wandered over to one of the café's picnic tables outside in the shade and took in the scene around her.

The café stood on the corner of an intersection flanked on all sides by rolling farm fields. Behind her was a fenced pasture with a large barn painted black. Two horses strolled lazily side by side, grazing on the famed Kentucky bluegrass.

Macy loved Lexington with all her heart. She had been so happy here for so many years. True, she had been lonely at times, and work had consumed much of her life, but it was hard not to smile as you drove along country roads with newborn Thoroughbred foals running in their fields alongside. It was a horse lover's paradise, and she liked that even now, more than a decade later, little had changed.

She loved the Windy Corner, sister restaurant to the more well-known Wallace Station, so she was glad that Adam had suggested it. Its menu consisted mostly of breakfast, salads, and sandwiches, but not only was the food excellent, but it was served with a smile. She was so lost in her revelry that she didn't even notice that Adam had pulled up.

"Daydreaming?" He asked and then laughed when she jumped.

"That's exactly what I was doing – you got me." She stood up from the table and gave Adam a hug.

"How's my girl?" He asked softly, holding her close and planting a kiss on her head.

"She's…okay. Being here makes my heart ache. I miss it so much, but I'm also reminded of why I left."

"I'm sorry." Adam held her tight for a few more minutes. "Let's go get something to eat and sit outside and enjoy the view."

A few minutes later, armed with heaping helpings of chicken salad and French fries, they were seated back outside under the shade of an old oak tree.

"Do you ever play the 'year ago' game? Well, it's not a game exactly, it's just something I do to torture myself." When Adam shook his head, she continued. "Well, my mom passed away last August, so it's been less than a year. So, every so often I think to myself, a year ago today, everything was fine. Everything was wonderful. And I think about what I was doing at that particular time, and it makes me mad that I didn't realize how good I had it. I wish I had been happier because life then was…perfect. And I'll never have that again."

"I used to think like that after my marriage began to suffer. I'd think about the early days and how we were so happy. It's a sad game to play with yourself, but it's a good reminder to live in the moment and enjoy every single day. Because, as we've learned, things can always get worse."

"That's a good point. I was never one to live in the moment. I always thought days, weeks, years ahead. I'm a planner, for the most part. So is Molly. Erin was always more go-with-the-flow, and I envied her for it."

"Well maybe that's the lesson here – and not just for you, for me too, for everyone. Live in the moment. Don't take anyone or anything for granted."

"I just wish I had learned it *before* I lost my mom."

"I know. Hindsight is 20/20, as they say. And it's painful."

"I don't want to waste any more time. I don't want to have regrets. I know it's impossible to live a perfect life, to always do and say the right things – you know? But I want to try. I don't want to lose anyone else and look back with regrets. I wish I had been more present when I was with my mom – my dad too. Instead I was always thinking about something else – horses, showing, college, work."

"Don't beat yourself up. You were just a kid when you lost your dad. And with your mom, I'm sure she wouldn't have changed a thing about you or your relationship with her. I'm sure she didn't like that you lived out of state, but I'm sure she *loved* that you were a horse vet, that you had followed your dreams, accomplished all your goals, and that you were happy. Because you were. I'm not a parent, but if I had kids, all I'd want is for them to be happy. No matter what they were doing or what they became in life, I'd just want them to be happy."

Tears had filled Macy's eyes and were threatening to overflow. "Thanks for that. I think you're right. All she ever wanted for me and Tommy was for us to be happy. Thanks for helping me see that. I still feel so guilty for all the time I had spent away, but I know my mom was proud of me."

"I'm certain she was. Everyone who knows you and what you've accomplished already in life is proud of you."

"Why are you so good to me when all I've been is crazy to you?"

"Why? Because I'm in love with you."

~ Chapter 36 ~

"Did you say it back?" Asked Erin as the two girls were huddled around the TV in the family room. They'd been watching the Kentucky Derby coverage all day and shrieking every time they spotted Adam.

After driving back east with Cassidy, getting her settled into her new apartment, and then jetting back home to work, this was the first time Macy and Erin had had a chance to catch up.

"No, I didn't. But I will. I want to."

"When will you say it?"

"When the time's right. It's almost right – I'm getting there. Adam won't rush it, he wants it to be right too."

"I'm just glad you two worked things out. He's way too handsome to let go."

Macy laughed. "That he certainly is. And he looks so dapper in his suit right now!"

"I wish you could have gone. Going to the Derby has been on my bucket list for so long."

"I wish I could be there too, but I promised Beau I'd be here to work." Molly and Beau were taking a second honeymoon since their original one had been cut short by Hadley's tragic death. Macy was happy they were finally getting to take the trip they deserved.

"Okay, here we go – they're loading into the starting gate," said Erin. The two inched even closer to the TV.

"My heart is pounding!"

"Mine too!" Said Erin as she grabbed Macy's hand. The two girls watched as the horses broke from the gate. *And they're off in the Kentucky Derby!*

Etch had drawn post position 15, which had

pleased Adam immensely. In a large field like the Derby, the largest field any of these horses would ever run in, the farther your horse can get from the rail, the better.

"He's in 4th. He's settling in nicely, just off the pace," said Macy, pointing at the screen. "That's it boy, nice and easy. Just stalk the frontrunner for a bit. Wait until the top of the stretch."

The horses thundered down the backstretch and Etch held his position firmly. His ears were pricked forward in anticipation. His jockey sat chilly, hardly moving or pumping his arms. All these were great signs. They were just waiting for the right time to make their move.

"AND THEY'RE INTO THE STRETCH, AND ETCH A SKETCH IS MAKING HIS MOVE!" Shouted Larry Collmus who was calling the race.

Macy and Erin bounded to their feet and pumped their arms as if they were riding the horse themselves.

"GO ETCH, GO!"

"HOLD ON ETCH, YOU'VE GOT THIS!"

"AND ETCH A SKETCH IS PULLING AWAY! HE'S AHEAD BY ONE...NOW TWO LENGTHS...THREE LENGTHS AND HE'S UNDER THE WIRE!"

"HE WON! WE WON!" Shouted the girls as they jumped up and down and hugged each other. "HE WON THE KENTUCKY DERBY!"

The TV cameras immediately panned from the track back into the sea of people in the grandstands, cheering, going wild, high-fiving one another, and waving their winning tickets.

A reporter caught up with Adam as he made his way down to the track towards the Winner's Circle.

"Adam, you just won the Kentucky Derby – how do you feel?!" Asked the reporter, shoving the microphone in front of Adam.

"I feel amazing. What a great horse – wasn't he just spectacular? The only thing that would have made this day better is having my beautiful girlfriend Macy by my side. I love you, Mace, wish you could have made it today."

Erin, smiling from ear to ear, reached over and grabbed her friend's hand. Macy just starred at the screen with tears streaming down her cheeks. "This is incredible, Mace."

Nodding her head and overcome by emotion, Macy whispered back. "He's incredible. I can't wait for him to come home."

~ The End ~

~ Acknowledgements ~

Novel #2 is in the books! I still can't believe I finished one book, much less two! To my readers – I couldn't do this without your kind words and support – thank you!

Thank you to Kay Yeager, Helen Parker, Kim Gerhardt, and Sylvia Berglie for continuously asking "How's that second book coming?" I truly appreciated the encouragement!

Mary Miller – my racehorse naming expert! I love that I can send you a quick text saying, "Help! I need racehorse names!" And you can immediately fire back with more than I need. Etch A Sketch was my favorite. Thank you!

Carly Kade – I so appreciate your wisdom, advice, and encouraging emails, and I love our growing partnership! #authorsunite!

And James – as always, you are my inspiration. You always go after what you want in life, and I love how you push me to do the same. You make me feel like my little writing career is the most important thing in the world. I love you.

~ About the Author ~

Laurie Berglie lives in Maryland with her husband, James, and their 7 four-legged children. She enjoys renovating her fixer-upper farm, reading horse books, and competing in the hunters. She has a BA in English from Stevenson University and an MA in Humanities from Towson University.

For more information, please visit: www.laurieberglie.com or her blog at www.themarylandequestrian.com. You can also find her on Instagram @marylandequestrian.

If you liked this book, please write a review on Amazon or Goodreads! Thank you!

Made in the USA
Columbia, SC
03 July 2020

13126174R00138